# Journey
## INTO
# Intimacy

EXPERIENCING THE DEPTH OF GOD'S LOVE

# STEVE MCVEY

**Journey into Intimacy**
Copyright ©2009 Steve McVey
All rights reserved

Cover Design by Pine Hill Graphics
Interior Design by Pine Hill Graphics

ISBN 978-0-9664736-1-2

# Contents

# SLOW DOWN AND ENJOY THE JOURNEY

# DAY ONE

## Preparing For The Journey

The next eight weeks might prove to be among the most valuable weeks of your Christian life. I don't make that statement just to get you hyped up about the study you are about to begin. I tell you that because it's true.

This study you are beginning can be compared to a journey toward intimacy with your Heavenly Father. The destination you will move toward is the place where you will experience a sense of His love in a greater way than you have known until now. While it's true that our Christian life isn't based on feelings, it is also true that no meaningful relationship we have doesn't include emotions too.

I can't imagine not knowing feelings as a part of the relationship I have with my wife, Melanie. Without emotions, our relationship would seem dry and academic instead of passionate and vibrant. That's sort of the way it is with your relationship to Christ. The Bible calls us His bride. Can you imagine a bride not having any emotions about her groom? Don't let anybody fool you – feelings are important.

### FEELINGS AREN'T FUNDAMENTAL, BUT THEY ARE STILL IMPORTANT

You may have heard teaching that so strongly cautioned you about the importance of not living by feelings that the whole idea of experiencing God's love at an emotional level is a little intimidating to you. None of us want to go off the deep end, but at the same time every one of us yearns for an experiential sense of our Father's love. That's where feelings come into focus. In an attempt not to live by feelings, many Christians have thrown out the baby with the bath water.

The fact is that every Christian has feelings related to their relationship to God. Many have negative feelings. Some feel frustrated. Others feel discouraged. Still others feel hopeless that they can ever experience that "first love" they knew when they first trusted Christ.

Others have positive feelings. Some feel peaceful. Some feel joyful. Others feel accepted and loved.

> *Be honest with yourself about where you are in terms of intimacy with God.*

Can we begin this walk into spiritual intimacy in agreement that you will be honest with yourself about where you are in terms of intimacy with God in your own Christian walk? Wherever you are right now, your Father will meet you there and will guide you into intimacy *if* you will be honest. Will you?

Before you go any further, stop here for a minute and write a short description of the feelings you experience in your relationship to God at this point in your life. Be sure not to write a description of what you *think*. That's how some people, who have trouble identifying feelings, respond to this type exercise. They might say, "I feel like..." and then tell what they *think*. Complete this sentence:

In my relationship to God, I *feel*: (not I feel *like*...)

_____

It's okay if you didn't say very much. I only want you to begin to identify how you describe the feelings of intimacy you have in your relationship to God as you start this journey. Some Christians are so out of touch with their feelings that they can't come up with anything. If you had a hard time identifying how you feel in your relationship to God, know that your experience isn't so uncommon. Be encouraged to know that feelings will grow within you as you increasingly discover the depths of your Father's love over the weeks to come.

Having a real hunger to experience an awareness of intimacy with your heavenly Father is necessary if you want to move one inch toward the destination of an intimate relationship to Him. If you sincerely want to feel your Father's embrace and know His love at the deepest level of your being, that's all it takes to start this journey.

This study will be built on a progression of truths that will set you free to experience intimacy with God. You can view the truths that are the focus of this eight-week study like mile markers that show the progress you are making toward your destination. With each passing week, you will become more aware of His love for you and you'll find yourself responding with eagerness to know Him even more fully.

These truths are meant to affect both your mind and your feelings. The life and love of Jesus Christ is intended to fill your whole being, not just certain parts of it. His desire is that the loving presence of His Life which lives in your spirit will spill over into your soul (mind, emotions, and will) and flood your life so that your actions will become an expression of Divine Love toward everybody you meet.

## THE KEY TO LOVING HIM MORE

For years I prayed, asking the Lord to help me to love Him more. As I have grown spiritually, I have come to realize an important key to loving Him more. "We love Him because He first loved us" (1 John 4:19). Based on what that verse says, what is it that we need to understand in order to love God the way our hearts long to do?

> *We love Him because He first loved us.*

_____

_____

I hope you gave the correct answer. The key to loving God more is to know how much He loves us. As we grow in our understanding of His love, we will respond by loving Him more. The depths of His love will be the main focus of your study during the next eight weeks. By the time you finish this study, you will know without a doubt that your Father totally loves you, just as you are. As a result of this knowledge, you'll find yourself loving Him more than ever.

*Week One*

Do you want a more intimate walk with God? Do you sense a yearning deep within you to experience a conscious intimacy with Him that runs deeper than every other experience of life? I think you do. That's why you decided to be a part of this study.

Your very desire for God is an act of His grace operating in you. Many people have no hunger to experience God in the way you want. If you have any doubt about your own hunger, the question has to be raised as to why you would even take the time to do this study. You *do* hunger for Him.

What makes you want to experience intimacy with God? It isn't because deep down you're a better person than a lot of people. It's because He has miraculously placed that hunger there so that He can then satisfy it. In other words, your hunger to know God intimately is proof that He is working in your life already and, make no mistake about it; God will finish what He starts. "For I am confident of this very thing, that He who began a good work in you will perfect it until the day of Christ Jesus" (Philippians 1:6).

> *What makes you want to experience intimacy with God?*

It is my prayer that in the weeks to follow you will see God's love from a perspective and to an extent that you may not have seen it until now. As you read the pages in this book, be mindful of the fact that no description of His love for the Christian can be exaggerated. To the contrary, "[His] lovingkindness is great to the heavens and [His] truth to the clouds" (Psalms 57:10). "I love you *this much!*" God says to you as He stretches out His arms across the clouds.

How would you describe God's love, as you understand it at this point in your life?

_____

_____

Infinite love can never be fully described using finite words, but the Holy Spirit can speak to us beyond the medium of words. It is my prayer that God will say more to you than this book can possibly say. You may find it to be very helpful in progressing through these pages if you will put aside your preconceived ideas about God's love and imagine that you are a blank page, waiting for His Spirit to write a love letter in your heart.

However big you imagine God's love for you to be, it is bigger. Open your heart and mind now to receive what He wants to reveal and say to you. The only preparation you need for this journey into intimacy is a desire to know Him. Allow your journey through these pages to be, not only an exercise of the mind, but also a journey of the heart. Be open to the possibility of having both your thoughts *and* emotions stimulated by the Holy Spirit. May your God-given faith and hunger lovingly push you toward a greater awareness of His passion for you until you are love struck in such a way that you never get over it – not for all eternity.

As you end today's reading, the first step in this eight week journey, use the following space to write a prayer to your Father, telling Him what you hope He will do in your life in regard to your sense of intimacy with Him. Remember to be honest. Tell Him how you feel right now and ask Him to awaken you to an understanding and awareness of His love that will affect you both in your intellect and in your emotions. Tell Him what you honestly think and feel. He longs for that kind of sincerity from those He loves. Once you have done this, you are fully prepared to move forward in this Jesus journey.

*Dear Father,*

_____

_____

_____

_____

_____

In Jesus Name,

*Amen.*

As you go through your day, reflect on your prayer and imagine what it will be like when your Father answers the prayer. You can be assured of one thing – He will.

*Week One*

# DAY TWO

## Don't Act Like Lucy

One of the biggest reasons why so many Christians don't sense the kind of intimacy with God they want to know has to do with the fact that they are on the wrong road altogether. Many have been misdirected from intimacy with Christ by the frenzied lifestyles they live. The lifestyles most of us live put so many demands on our time and attention that we simply have nothing left to give to our pursuit of spiritual things.

It is ironic that, although we live in a day when we have more time saving devices than any generation in history has ever possessed, we somehow find ourselves more driven by our schedules than anybody before us could have imagined. I don't want to sound negative at this point, but complete honesty is required here. If you really want to consciously experience a sense of intimacy with your heavenly Father, it is likely that you may need to restructure your priorities in order to get on the right road toward intimacy.

Growing in any love relationship requires focused attention. It isn't something that happens incidentally while we rush through life at breakneck speed. This reality is true whether it's a relationship with a friend, your mate or your God.

Do you remember the kind of intimacy you experienced with Jesus Christ when you first became a Christian? In the following space, describe what it was like then:

_____

_____

_____

I've asked you to describe the intimacy you shared with Christ then in hopes that thinking about it will cause you to long to know that kind of intimacy again. Many who once knew a conscious sense of intimacy with God have lost it. It didn't happen through an act of defiance. Instead it was lost through an attitude of *duty*.

They became so preoccupied with duties at home, at work and at church that somehow the love affair they once enjoyed with Jesus simply faded. They have unknowingly veered off the main road of the grace walk, which is living in conscious union with God. Ask these Christians today if they love the Lord and without hesitation they will affirm that they do. Ask them if they are experiencing the kind of intimate relationship with Jesus they once knew, and they will be forced to admit that things have changed.

> *It isn't because most Christians don't love Jesus that they have lost their sense of intimacy with Him.*

They aren't unlike the young mom who responded to her husband's complaint that she never wanted to make love to him anymore with the admission, "I'm just too tired." It isn't because most Christians don't love Jesus that they have lost their sense of intimacy with Him. It's just that they have become focused on so many other things that they simply don't have any energy left for Him.

A few years ago, when I found myself at a place where I had allowed the demands of my lifestyle to distract me from the deep awareness of abiding in my Father's love, I wrote the following words in my personal journal. See if you can identify with my frustration at wandering on a side road that God never intended I travel. (The reference is from the old "I Love Lucy" TV show.)

*"I feel like Lucy Ricardo working on the production line at the candy factory. I can't keep up and I can't swallow anymore. What is God showing me to do? I believe that He is redirecting my life and ministry to focus on the*

*Week One*

*things He has called me to and not to become distracted by lesser, albeit good, things.*

*I need to remember that bigger is not necessarily better, that to be busier isn't necessarily to be more productive. I need to learn that I don't have to say yes to every "great opportunity" that comes along.*

*I want to grow in my knowledge of God and His ways. I want to experience greater intimacy with Him. I want to be obsessed with Him so that the things that don't matter won't matter. I want to be inwardly at rest. I want my mind to stop whirling all the time with thoughts, plans and ideas. I want to be able to relax mentally and to feel an emotional calmness by default. I want to cry with joy over God's manifest presence."*

## ACTIONS SPEAK LOUDER THAN WORDS

Think about your lifestyle for a moment. How do you spend your time? Does your investment of time and energy accurately reflect the value you place on those things? Or do you find yourself giving more to some things than they deserve?

*Does your investment of time and energy accurately reflect the value you place on those things?*

To progress in your own journey into intimacy with your Father, it is necessary to identify which road you are traveling in life right now. Maybe you have lost your way and need to be pointed to the right route again. If you're headed in the wrong direction with your time and energy, it is important to recognize that fact so that a course correction can occur.

I'd like for you to pause and look at the road signs around you. Perhaps this will help you realize where you are in your own journey. Think about your lifestyle for a moment. What are the areas in life where you spend most of your time and energy?

1. _____

2. _____

3. _____

4. _____

5. _____


Do your answers reveal anything to you about where you are in life? Judging by your answers, what does the evidence indicate are the most important areas of your life? Do your priorities align with the hunger in your heart to live from a foundation of faith in Christ?

The list above isn't intended to cause you to feel self-condemnation. Your Father doesn't condemn you at all. (See Romans 8:1) Instead, this list may be what the Holy Spirit will use as road signs to indicate where you are presently headed.

It isn't that there aren't many important things in life. There are. A key for the Christian is in learning to keep all things in the proper perspective.

> *Your Father doesn't condemn you at all.*

You are probably familiar with the story of Mary and Martha in Luke 10:38-42. The Bible says, "Martha was distracted with much service" (10:40). This is an important issue to see, so I ask you this question to make sure that you get the point here.


From whom was she distracted? _____


What caused her to be distracted? _____


Martha wasn't involved in bad behavior. Her actions were good and respectable, yet she was distracted *from Jesus*. The thing that caused her to become distracted was *service*.

There is certainly nothing wrong with fulfilling the responsibilities in life to which God has called us. The trouble comes either when we take on things that we haven't been led by God to carry or when we allow ourselves to be defined by what we do, instead of Whose we are.

Martha's problem was one of priority. Jesus lovingly pointed out to her that she was uptight and filled with anxiety because she didn't understand an important and foundational matter of life for those who know Him.

## One Thing

Some might say that she needed to learn balance, but that isn't what Jesus said. He told her that there is only *one thing* that ultimately matters in life. That thing is living out of our union with Him. Everything else is to flow out of that. I mentioned earlier that there are many important things in life, but their importance is directly connected to how they relate to Christ.

Despite what many may have believed, the great need in our lives is not to learn balance, putting Jesus first. Jesus isn't just first. He is everything. He is to be the source that animates our every action in every area of our lives. *One* thing is important – allowing your relationship to Christ to be the foundation upon which everything else in your lifestyle is built.

As Martha experienced, the subtle robbery of intimacy with Christ has occurred with many Christians, not because they are insincere about their faith, but because they have focused on doing all the right things in life to the exclusion of living out of intimacy that comes from our spiritual union with Him. Somehow along the way their heavenly Father has been pushed to the back of the line.

As you look at the list of things that occupy your time and energy, it is doubtful that you have listed things that are inherently wrong. The problem comes when we fail to realize that everything we do in life is to be an expression and extension of Christ's life that resides within us.

## Seeking Him First

> *Everything else falls in perfect alignment when we seek Him first.*

Matthew 6:33 says, "Seek [God's] kingdom first and His righteousness and all these things will be added to you." Everything else falls in perfect alignment when we seek Him first. In what way would a person "seek God's kingdom first?" Contrary to what you may have heard in the past, this verse isn't talking about going to church more or increasing any other level of religious activity in your life. In fact, at times those may even be a deterrent to growing in intimacy.

If you are on the wrong road, the answer isn't to drive faster by increasing what you're doing. The need is to get off the wrong road. If you're going the wrong direction, it doesn't matter how fast you drive. You will never reach your destination.

Take a second look at your list and answer the following questions:

1. In what ways are you trusting Christ to express His life through you in these areas?

_____

2. Do the things on your list need to be rearranged in order to reflect their importance?

_____

3. Is there anything on your list that needs to be removed?

_____

4. Are there items not listed here that you realize would be added to the list if you were to begin to live in a way that truly reflects what is most important to you?

_____

The purpose for asking you to make the list and answer these questions is in no way intended to cause you to feel guilty or sense a need to improve yourself. The purpose is for you to open yourself to God's Spirit in an honest way. If you see areas where there is a need for change, that recognition in no way is a call to you to embark on a self-improvement program.

> *In what ways are you trusting Christ?*

To the contrary, the invitation is for you to recognize that navigating your own lifestyle has robbed you of the intimacy with God that you want and to cause you to yield yourself completely to Him, asking Him to teach you how to order your days so that your time and energy will be animated by His indwelling Life in such a way that you will experience the abundant life which is your birthright as a Christian. (See John 10:10)

As you end today's study, pause and pray, talking to the Lord about the things you have listed which consume your days. Ask Him if you have been sidetracked in life. Surrender each area of life to Him. Ask Him to move in you, causing your daily activities to reflect who you truly are at the deepest level of your being. Acknowledge your willingness to give up being the navigator of your lifestyle. Ask Him to take the wheel and begin to direct you onto the road He wants you to travel.

# DAY THREE

## Recognizing the Roadblocks

*E*ven though we may have good intentions, it is possible to hit road-blocks in our journey toward intimacy with our Father. In my case, I love being busy. When I go on vacation, it usually takes me a few days just to settle down and arrive emotionally and mentally at our destination. Even at home, I find it hard to sit still and do nothing. Sometimes my wife, Melanie, will watch me pacing from the computer to the television to the couch and back to the computer and will finally say, "Will you perch somewhere?"

I tend to thrive on activity. People often applaud that kind of attitude. Folks like me are seldom called lazy. "Insensitive," sometimes. "Driven," yes. "Impatient," without a doubt. But one thing is sure, we get things done, whether they need to get done or not.

### MY WAKE UP CALL

A few years ago I went to a cabin in the country four days ahead of a scheduled conference where I was to speak. My plan was to use the time to write a magazine article I had been asked to do and to work on another book, whose deadline crunch six months away I was beginning to feel more and more. Yet as I tried to write, my thoughts were deadlocked. "What's going on Lord?" I asked. "You know that I have planned this time to write." Someone rightly said that if you want to make God laugh, tell Him *your* plans. I'm sure I must have made Him snicker that day. You've heard of writer's block? I was at the literary Great Wall of China.

Sitting alone in the country cabin, I began to read an article from a magazine someone had left there. The author was recounting a scene from the movie *Coal Miner's Daughter*. She described a scene in which Loretta Lynn is on stage. A Loretta who did way too much, too soon, too fast. On the verge of a breakdown and wiping at a free fall of tears, she told her beloved fans, "Patsy Cline used to tell me, 'Little gal – you got to run your own life!' But I can tell you, my friends, right now, my life's a-runnin' me."

As I read the article, my emotions were stirred. I knew how she felt. At the same time, I found it mildly amusing that God seemed to be speaking to me through the words of Patsy Cline and Loretta Lynn, since I've never been a big fan of country music. "My life's a-runnin' me." The words kept echoing in my mind all night.

I had traveled around the world; speaking and I loved what I was doing. Who could argue with my activity? After all, it was *good* things that occupied my time. (Remember studying Martha as you read yesterday?)

> *It was Christian ministry that became a roadblock hindering my sense of intimacy with Christ.*

Does it strike you as strange that it was Christian ministry that became a roadblock hindering my sense of intimacy with Christ? I unknowingly had begun to love the work of the ministry more than the One who had called me into ministry. The enemy of our souls is so subtle and sneaky!

Think about your lifestyle for a moment. What is the thing in your own life that could most likely become a roadblock against your sense of intimacy with God? It probably isn't a "bad thing." Where are you most vulnerable?

_____

The day came in my life when something that seemed insignificant at the time happened. I woke up with an itchy scalp caused by a rash. After a few days, it went away and I thought no more about it. A short time later the same kind of rash showed up on my ankle. It went away again only to show up another time on my calf. After seeing this burning irritant come this many times, I finally went to the doctor. He took one look at it and said, "Tell me about your lifestyle." "What do you mean?" I asked. "Is your work stressful?" he asked. "I love what I do," I responded. "That doesn't mean it isn't stressful," he answered. Then my doctor proceeded to announce that this persistent rash was the result of nothing other than stress. Stress? Not a good diagnosis for a man who teaches others how to rest in Christ.

If you have read my book, *A Divine Invitation*, you know how this personal story progressed. Suffice it to say that between Loretta Lynn, an itchy rash accompanied by a doctor's blunt diagnosis, and my repeated scatter-brained reactions to life, I saw that something was wrong.

## THE SMALL, STILL VOICE

When we allow ourselves to get so caught up in our daily routine that it becomes a roadblock that obscures our ability to see the face of Jesus Christ, the Holy Spirit within us doesn't ignore that fact. He begins to speak to us, softly at first (like through my absentmindedness), and then continues to speak louder (the rash on my scalp and leg) to get our attention. He will even use the mundane events of our lives (reading a story about Loretta Lynn) to make us aware of our wandering ways.

God still speaks to those He loves today. We will look more in depth at that in your seventh week of study. Jesus said, "My sheep hear my voice" (John 10:27). Make no mistake about it; He speaks to you in your own life. Your God is not mute.

Think about your own life experiences. Have there been times when your focus on Christ was blocked because you were distracted by other things? What are some ways that God spoke to you to make you aware of what was happening in your life?

> *God still speaks to those He loves today.*

_____

_____

Maybe He spoke to you through something that somebody else said (often our mates), or maybe it was through something physical (a rash, migraines, stomach problems, etc.). Perhaps he spoke to you through negative emotions (frustration, tension, depression). It could have been through something you read. It might have been a growing awareness that something wasn't in order in your life.

I have asked you to identify some ways that you have recognized your Father's voice because I want you to see that, when our sense of intimacy with Christ wanes, there will always be *something* He uses to get our attention. Do you recognize how He has spoken in your life?

> ## All Christians know that our Father speaks to us through the Bible.

All Christians know that our Father speaks to us through the Bible, but He also speaks in other ways. Of course, none of them will contradict His written Word, but we may certainly hear Him speak through these various means. For instance, you have probably heard the voice of God through a sermon, a song, a Christian friend, a book you have read, etc.

Think about the ways that God spoke in the Bible. Can you think of three ways that He spoke to people in Scripture?

1. _____

2. _____

3. _____

The purpose for this question is to help awaken you to the fact that we don't serve a silent God who is removed from our daily lifestyles. He is intimately interested and involved in the details of your life and wants to speak to you consistently through many means. This fact doesn't diminish your Bible; it magnifies your God!

As you move through these weeks of study, be assured that your heavenly Father plans to speak to you. He will speak through the content of this book and through the Bible verses discussed here. It is important to know that He will likely speak to you apart from your time studying the content of this book.

You have begun a journey in which you are progressing 24 hours a day. As you move ahead in your pursuit of intimacy with your Father, keep your eyes and ears opened to see and hear Him as He reveals His love to you in the daily details of your lifestyle.

End your study today by acknowledging to Him the ways that you have heard Him speak to you in the past. Express your heart's desire to become more sensitized to hearing His voice in the day-to-day details of your life.

*Dear Father,*

_____

_____

_____

_____

_____

_____

In Jesus name,

*Amen.*

Now, go through your day with your eyes and ears wide open!

# DAY FOUR

## *It's All About Knowing Him, Not Doing For Him*

*D*o you remember reading the description I gave a few days ago of how I had felt like Lucy working in the candy factory? I was so busy I could barely keep up with the demands on my time. I felt a constant sense of underlying frustration. I felt hurried, frenzied, scattered. Can you relate?

How would you describe the way you have felt, in terms of your schedule and the demands on your own time?

_____

_____

_____

Reading the words that I had written, my problem became clear to me. I was hungry to experience deep intimacy with Jesus Christ, but had become distracted by my busy lifestyle. Do you find the same to be true in your life? As a person who spends my full time in ministry, I had allowed the mechanics of "living a Christian life" to suffocate the exhilarating awareness of the indwelling presence of Christ. The enemy had used his classic weapon against me – causing me to focus more on "the Christian life" than on Christ Himself. I sincerely loved the Lord, but had temporarily lost that sense of intimate union known only by those who are *in love* with Jesus.

The specifics of our circumstances are probably different, but most of us in the modern church face the same basic temptation ~ letting ourselves get so busy with life that we miss the promised abundance of *the Life* that God has given us. (See John 10:10). God has chosen you to be His bride for a specific reason. He wants to pour out His love on you. Have you allowed yourself to miss out on the experiential awareness of the abundant life Christ has given you? If you sincerely want to experience intimacy with God, it may be necessary to rearrange some things in your lifestyle. I don't tell you that to make you feel guilty. It's just the way it is.

## KNOWING GOD

Read John 17:3 in your Bible. What did Jesus say is the meaning of eternal life? "This is eternal life – that they might _____ _____." The word "know" is the same one used by the mother of Jesus when she questioned the angel's announcement of her giving birth to a son by saying, "How can this be, since I *know* no man?" The word denotes experiential intimacy with someone. God saved you because He wants to *know* you. He is consumed with a resolve to love you like you've never been loved before, with an intensity and commitment greater than you can possibly imagine.

Since God's greatest desire toward His bride is for us to really know how much He loves us, it makes sense that the Devil's greatest mission would be to prevent us from experiencing that love. If a frontal attack from the Enemy can't make us turn away from Jesus Christ by seducing us back to the world, He will utilize another battle plan. He will cause us to become preoccupied with everything else, in fact, with *anything* else, other than Jesus Christ.

> *God saved you because He wants to know you.*

Many believers have been taken prisoners of war through a covert attack from hell and, the saddest part of it is, they don't even know it. They are being held captive in a prison of busyness. They sincerely desire to advance spiritually and often wonder why they aren't making more progress. They don't know that the reason all they seem to do is to walk in circles is because that is all anybody in a prison cell *can* do.

*Week One*

The ongoing awareness of His indwelling life as our own isn't something that causes us to grit our teeth and determine to practice. It is an underlying state of *resting in Christ* at all times. To rest in Him means that we totally depend on Christ as our life source at every moment and in every situation. It is the default setting of anybody who is living out of the union he shares with God through Jesus Christ.

Do you remember when you first became a believer how *obsessed* you were with Jesus Christ? Even when you weren't consciously thinking about Him, the reality of His presence rested just beneath your conscious thoughts. For the first time, you were aware that He was there, inside you, loved you in a way you had never known love until then. With the slightest prompting, you would find yourself whispering a prayer, witnessing to a friend, thinking of Jesus and what He meant to you.

> *To rest in Him means that we totally depend on Christ.*

Many who once knew the reality of that kind of faith have lost it. They didn't lose it through an act of defiance. Instead it was lost through an attitude of *duty*. They became so preoccupied with duties at home, at work and at church that somehow the love affair they once enjoyed with Jesus simply faded. Ask these today if they love the Lord and without hesitation they will tell you that they do. Ask them if they are experiencing the kind of intimate relationship with Jesus they once knew, and they will be forced to admit that things have changed.

"So what's wrong with the fact that I've been busy with my Christian duties?" somebody may ask. The Apostle Paul answers: "If I have the gift of prophecy, and know all mysteries and all knowledge; and if I have all faith, so as to remove mountains, but do not have love, I am nothing. And if I give all my possessions to feed the poor, and if I deliver my body to be burned, but do not have love, it profits me nothing" (1 Corinthians 13:2-3). So much for "Christian service" separated from a love relationship.

"Are you suggesting that we owe God *nothing* at all, after all that He has done for us?" one pastor asked me. "Kurt, what *could* you owe God for all that He has done for you?" I asked. "How could we ever repay God for a priceless gift?" "Of course, I know we could never repay Him," Kurt said. "But we can spend our lives *trying* to repay Him," "And *how* do we do that?" I persisted. "What could we offer God that would even *begin* to repay Him for His goodness to us?" Kurt's perspective isn't an uncommon one, but my question to him demands an answer. How could we ever repay God for His great gift of eternal life in Jesus Christ?

Are there things you have done to try to repay God for all He has done for you? What are they?

1._____

2._____

3._____

4._____

To what extent would you have to do these things and how long would you have to do them until you repaid Him? Of course, the whole concept is foreign to grace.

The word "gospel" means "good news." Here's the best part of the good news – you don't have to try to repay God. God's desire for you is that you will grow in your knowledge of and capacity to receive His love. Forget what you think you owe Him and accept, by faith that it has already been paid.

As you end your reading today, talk to your Father about your schedule. If you see things that consume too much of your time, tell Him about it. Acknowledge the foolishness of ways you may have tried to repay Him for His grace. Ask Him to show you the deterrents in your daily routine that rob you of being constantly aware of His love for you. Don't make any promises. Just be honest with Him about where you are in your journey at this point.

*Dear Father,*

_____

_____

_____

_____

_____

_____

*Amen.*

    Go forward into your day trusting Him to gently show you how to spend your time and energy. You can be encouraged to know that the burden for change in your life is on Him, not you. Your role is simply to trust Him to accomplish all that He wants to do in your life.

# DAY FIVE

## *Learning To Relax*

*W*e've spent the better part of this week considering how we tend to allow the daily demands of our schedules to rob us of a sense of intimacy with Christ. Yesterday, we considered how we sometimes get caught up in religious activity in an attempt to repay God for His goodness toward us. Today, let's take that a little further.

### IT'S RIDICULOUS TO TRY TO REPAY SOME DEBTS

Adam and Joshua were in Iraq together, often fighting side by side during intense skirmishes. One day Adam's unit pulled out and he was stuck in a spot alone and under severe attack. He had been wounded and wasn't able to stand to his feet. Upon discovering what had happened, Joshua rushed back into the heat of the conflict, battled his way to the foxhole where Adam laid without hope. Joshua threw him across his shoulders and began to run for safety. As he approached the protection of his own unit, Joshua was shot in the back. He collapsed forward into a foxhole, where his allies immediately cared for both he and Adam.

Joshua spent a month in the hospital, requiring back surgery and physical therapy. He had paid a great price to save his buddy. But to him, Adam was worth it. After all, they were best friends.

After they arrived back home, one day Joshua came home to find Adam putting his lawn mower back into his garage. "What are you doing?"

Joshua asked. "I just came over and mowed your lawn," Adam answered. "Why?" Joshua asked. "Well, I was thinking about it," Adam said. "You did save my life in Bagdad, and I thought that maybe I could try to repay you by cutting the grass for you."

How do you think Joshua would feel when Adam told him that? I confess that this event didn't really happen. I simply tell it to show how ridiculous it is to repay somebody who has sacrificed so greatly on our behalf with our own insignificant gestures. For Adam to think he could begin to repay Joshua by mowing the lawn would be absurd. Worse than that, it would be an insult to Joshua, who had risked his life for his friend. Joshua didn't save Adam's life to get his grass cut. He saved him because he loved his friend.

We are all born sons of Adam, yet our Joshua – Jesus Christ, has rescued believers. He didn't simply risk His life. He *gave* His life for us. What could we ever do to repay Him? There is nothing that we *can* do, except accept the fact that He loves us that much. Will His love make a difference in how we act? Of course it will! However, our behavior is the result of His actions toward us, not a repayment for them. Don't try to pay a price for a priceless gift. It only demonstrates that we have no concept of its infinite value. Worse yet, it is an insult to the One who gave the gift.

> *Don't try to pay a price for a priceless gift.*

When I was a legalistic pastor, I really pushed the idea of our owing God. "After all He has done for you" was the prod I used to keep the sheep moving. "After all He has done for you, and you can't come to church on Sunday night?" "After all He has done for you and you won't even tithe?" "After all He has done for you and you can't find the courage to witness to your neighbor?"

I was sincere in my attempt to motivate people *to do* more for Christ. I thought the answer for every need every Christian had was to do more. Read the Bible more. Pray more. Witness more. Give more. Go to church more. During those days, my last name should have been Moore instead of McVey.

Maybe you're a hard worker too. You might be an elder or deacon or another leader in your church. You might even be the pastor. My assumption is that you are very sincere about your Christian walk. Otherwise, you wouldn't be doing all the things you are doing.

Be sure that you note this statement before you continue reading what I have to say about "Christian service." *As Jesus Christ lives His life through us, we will actively serve God in supernatural ways.* Did you absorb what you just read? Go back and read that italicized sentence again. Underline it.

Do you know that the reason God saved you has nothing to do with Him needing you to serve Him? Consider Acts 17:25, where the Bible says about God, "nor is He served by human hands as though He needed anything." What does God need? _____

In Psalm 50:12, God said that if He were hungry, He wouldn't bother to tell you. Why? Because there would be nothing you could do about it.

Let's face it – God doesn't need us, not in the least. We need Him though – desperately. There is nothing you could ever do for God that He couldn't do for Himself, much more quickly, easily and efficiently.

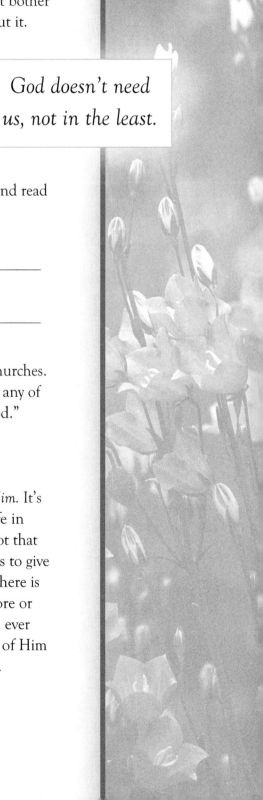

*God doesn't need us, not in the least.*

One time the disciples asked Jesus a question about working for God. They asked, "What shall we do that we might do the works of God?" (See John 6:28) Take your own Bible and read John 6:29 to see how Jesus answered. He said:

*This is the work of God, that you* _____

_____

That answer presents a problem for many modern Christians and churches. When Jesus defined "the work of God," He didn't say a word about any of the things that the modern church stresses as being the "work of God."

## THE WORK OF GOD

What is the work of God that He wants you to do? *Believe in Him.* It's that simple. Imagine a particular kind of life for a moment. It is a life in which God requires nothing from you. In this life, His purpose is not that you should try to give Him anything. He, on the other hand, intends to give you everything necessary for your complete fulfillment. In this life, there is nothing you could ever do that would cause God to love you any more or any less than He does right now. Imagine that nothing you do could ever change how God feels about you in even the slightest degree. Think of Him loving you with a passionate, unconditional love that will never end.

*Week One*

This life is not an imaginary one. It is real. As His bride, you are the one He has dreamed about for all eternity. The hopes and plans of Deity rest within you. Even if your past religious indoctrination or your sense of spiritual inadequacy causes your mind to resist the kind of life I've described, something deep within your spirit may resonate with this description of life. It is from that place that God wants you to live every day.

> *Christian service is the normal outflow through one who allows Jesus Christ to live through him.*

I've been in church long enough to know that this kind of talk scares some Christians. Every legalistic bone in their body cries out, "But the Bible *does* talk about the importance of service!" I never said it didn't. I'm simply saying that we live in an era where modern church life often stresses *doing* above everything else in the Christian life, and that is wrong – dead wrong. Christian service is the normal outflow through one who allows Jesus Christ to live through him. Religious activity is a counterfeit. The two are nothing alike.

If you want to slow down and enjoy the journey toward a deeper intimacy with your Heavenly Father, it will help you to know whether your actions are an expression of Christian service or religious activity. Which of the following describes your lifestyle?

| Religious Activity | Christian Service |
|---|---|
| Wears you down in every way. | Is invigorating and motivating. |
| Always leaves you feeling like you could have done better. | Leaves you feeling pleased and satisfied that you have glorified your Father. |
| Demands more and more. | Gives the contentment of a job well done. |
| Is often motivated by guilt or need. | Flows from a heart of love and desire. |
| Insists on a particular outcome. | Focuses on the joy of serving. |

Can you think of other differences between empty religious activity and authentic Christian service? What are they?

I assume that most people who read this book are Christians. I also assume you want to experience a greater sense of intimacy with God, or you wouldn't be taking the time to do this. It is on the basis of those assumptions that I lovingly say to you that doing more religious things is not going to help you reach your desired destination. In fact, it will hinder you.

Is it possible that you need to re-evaluate what you are doing "for God" and ask why you are doing those things? Is your activity an expression of His life from within you? Do you do those things because they are a sincere expression of love? Do you find joy in what you are doing?

I raise these questions because I am the poster-child for one who tried to find intimacy with God by doing more religious things. I lovingly implore you to learn from my many years of mistakes by taking my word on this matter – It won't work. Not now. Not ever.

> *Your need is not to do more for Christ. Your need is to slow down and enjoy the journey.*

Your need is not to do more for Christ. Your need is to *slow down and enjoy the journey*. He wants you to know Him intimately. As we move forward together through this study, you will discover more and more about Him and who He is. In the process, you are going to learn more about who you are too.

My purpose in what you are reading today isn't to discount serving Christ through your church. My goal is to help you see that if you work at church as a means to an end – that by working hard there, you will experience intimacy with God, it isn't going to work. Serving God in church is to be the overflow of intimacy that we already enjoy with Him, not a gateway to experience it. When you put the cart before the horse, you won't move an inch. You simply won't.

As you end this week of study, I pray that you can drive your first mile marker into the ground at this point in the journey. Why not end this week by writing a prayer to your Father? Tell Him specifically how you intend to respond to the Truth you have received from Him this week. Are you going to slow down and enjoy the journey? What changes do you trust Him to bring into your routine that will enable that to happen? How will this affect you at work? At church? In your spare time? Tell Him:

*Week One*

*Dear Father,*

_____

_____

_____

_____

_____

*Amen*

# Week Two

# LEAVE YOUR GUILTY CONSCIOUS AT HOME

## DAY ONE

# *God Hasn't Set You Aside*

*H*ave you heard about how some vindictive people have ruined the cars of somebody they had a grudge against by putting sugar in their gas tank? I've never had it happen to me, but my understanding is that it will permanently ruin a car's engine.

The enemy of our souls has done something similar to many Christians. He has introduced a foreign substance into their minds and emotions that has had the same damaging effect as sugar in an engine. What is this foreign matter that has brought so many Christians to a standstill in their journey toward intimacy? It is a guilty conscious.

Many believers have lost the forward momentum of their grace walk because of a nagging sense of guilt about things in their past or even things present in their lives today. If you think it would be a sinister thing to put sugar in somebody's gas tank, know without a doubt that Christians who have become paralyzed by a guilty conscience have suffered an experience much worse than having sugar put in an engine.

During our study this week, we are going to trust the Holy Spirit to address any sense of guilt you may have in your own life. This subject is early in your study for good reason. It's because once this has happened you'll find yourself accelerating toward intimacy with your heavenly Father at a faster speed than you have ever known.

We will consider the issue from different angles as the week progresses. Each one will move you further away from any guilt that may

*Week Two*

37

condemn you and bring you closer to seeing your Father's warm smile and experiencing His tender embrace.

## DISQUALIFIED FROM SERVICE

Some people think that they have committed so many sins or done something so bad that God couldn't possibly use their life or even feel toward them the same way He does toward those whose past is less spotted by sins. Nothing could be further from the truth. Allow me to give you an example from one person's life.

Someone recently told me a story about another person he knew very well. For many years of my life, the story he told me would have been very hard for me to understand because it contradicts much of what I had always believed.

> *Some people think that they have committed so many sins or done something so bad that God couldn't possibly use their life.*

John (I'll change his name to protect the guilty.) and his wife, Sarah, were taking a trip in a country outside the United States. John had professed to have known the Lord for a long time, having made a profession of faith and even had told his friends that he believed God was going to use his life in a big way.

One day he and his wife found themselves in a certain city at a place where they never should have gone to start with, to a place where they *wouldn't* have gone if they had been trusting in God at the moment. In some ways, what they did wasn't unique. Certainly, they aren't the only people who have ever gone out of town, been to some places and done some things they shouldn't do.

However, in this instance John soon found himself in over his head. His wife was a good-looking woman, and they weren't exactly in an environment where the fact that they were married mattered to anybody. He looked around and saw tough, crude, strong men there, the kind that often frequent sleazy bars on back streets in a bad part of town. It occurred to John that these characters wouldn't hesitate to do whatever they had to do to him for the chance to get at his wife. So John did the unthinkable – he told her to do whatever they asked. Maybe by doing what they wanted, the two of them could get out of this situation relatively unharmed.

Circumstances unfolded exactly as he had feared. My friend, who told me this story, said that John actually let his wife go home with one of these men, while he waited for her to return. More difficult to believe than what he did is that, after this situation happened, John continued on with his trip, still professing to love God and claiming to have a desire to follow Him. Some might say he couldn't really be a believer and act that way, but John is a minister who is considered by many people to be a great spiritual leader.

Think about this man for a moment? What are your thoughts about him?

_____

Is there any way that he could indeed be a spiritual leader? _____

I might add that what he did didn't stay hidden. Eventually, everybody found out about it. Everyone who knows about him knows about this incident. It is also noteworthy that this sin didn't happen before he came to the Lord. It happened afterwards, while he was professing to follow God's guidance for his life.

I encourage you to pause in your reading for a moment and identify in your own mind what you believe about this man's circumstances. Can God use him in ministry to others? Or did his actions permanently disqualify him from being used by God? Would you take spiritual advice from him? What would you say about the likelihood that God would ever use this man's life? Would it make any difference to you if I told you that later, on another occasion, he let his wife sleep with *another* man? It's true, he did. Knowing that, what do you think are his chances of being somebody who can ever have spiritual impact on others?

*Do our actions permanently disqualify us from being used by God?*

Allow me to explain the missing details of this incident. The Friend who told me the story about this man is the Holy Spirit. He told this story in the Bible in Genesis 12. As I relayed the story to you I called the man John, but his real name is Abraham. The story is about how he and Sarah traveled down to Egypt and committed this sin while they were there.

It is an amazing, if not confusing, aspect of God's grace that He will use a man like Abraham. Not only did God use him, but also in Hebrews 11, as if He has completely forgotten that He already gave us the low-down on the man in Genesis, the Holy Spirit lists Abraham as a *hero* of our faith. Most people wouldn't even recommend Abraham as "Husband Of The Year," but God lists him as a man of great faith. Apparently there is something about the way God judges people that is very different from the way most of us view others or ourselves. He looks past behavior and into the heart more readily than we can even imagine.

This kind of application is scary to many Christians. They're afraid when this kind of illustration is given that it will encourage sin in people's lives, but in reality most people don't need encouragement in order to sin. There is already an abundance of encouragement to sin in the world around us. If anybody decides to sin, including the Christian, we don't need encouragement to do it. People will sin with or without it.

*Most people don't need encouragement in order to sin.*

When we move from the world into the church, there is much encouragement about how *not* to sin. Most of us have been given list after list of suggestions about how to keep from sinning. The world encourages us to sin. The church encourages us not to sin. However, I don't find much encouragement anywhere for those who *have* sinned, which is all of us. Don't think you haven't sinned just because yours doesn't fall into the same category as Abraham's sin. Adultery is a horrible sin, but when I was a local church pastor for over twenty years, I saw a hundred times more damage done in the church by gossip and murmuring than I did by those who had committed adultery. It is easy to identify the "hall of shame" sins in the lives of others, yet be blind to the less obvious sins of our own lives.

There will always be those who look down their noses in judgment on the ones who have miserably failed. They are like the elder brother in the story of the prodigal son. They sneer at those who have foolishly sinned, despite the fact that, they too are miserable after faithfully serving. Licentiousness or legalism, they are two sides to the same performance based coin. They both produce the same dryness of soul that cries out for the miraculous outpouring of God's thirst quenching grace.

This week's study is not directed to those who are held captive by the most serious sin – that of not seeing their own sins. It is my prayer that the

Holy Spirit will give comfort and encouragement to Christians who *know* they have sinned. God's love for you is greater than your sins. Even if you have sinned in a big way, "where sin is big, God's grace is bigger!" I'll say it so plainly that it may sound shocking to a legalistic mind – you cannot out-sin the love of God!

I'll state this disclaimer one time, as clearly as I know how, in an attempt not to be misunderstood: It is not my intent to minimize the seriousness of sin in this chapter. Sin is a serious matter. It was for our sin that Christ went to the cross. However, this week's study isn't being written to keep people from sinning. It is addressed to those who have sinned and know it. It is written with the hope that the Holy Spirit will release them from self-condemnation and feelings of spiritual inferiority. Many believers have never enjoyed intimacy with God because they are continually held in bondage by shame over their past sins. My intention here is not to be soft on sin, but to be soft on people who are hurting! If you begin to think otherwise in reading this chapter, remind yourself of this particular paragraph.

Having tried to calm the fears of those who are afraid that undiluted grace may encourage sin, the studies for the rest of the week are for *you*, the one who has sinned and knows it. Jesus said that those who are well don't need a doctor, and that He can't help them. But those who have been infected by sin and need help are the ones He seeks. If you are like the overwhelming majority of Christians, you can point to incidents in your own past, or maybe even in your present behavior, about which you are ashamed. You should know that you are in good company.

> *Those who are well don't need a doctor.*

I won't ask you to write down your own sins that might have caused you to become paralyzed in your grace walk. I will, however, ask you to stop right here for a moment and think about them...Do you have them in your mind? I ask you now to mentally take those sins and imagine laying them at the foot of the cross of Jesus Christ. I assure you they were put away there.

## AN UNLIKELY HALL OF FAME

Hebrews 11 lists people that God considers as role models for the community of faith. A quick glance at the names mentioned there might lead to the conclusion that God isn't very picky about whom He is willing to use. If the modern church were to form a list like that, we probably wouldn't have included many of those mentioned in that chapter. Or, if we had decided to list their names, at least we would have left out some of the gory details of the inconsistent and filthy behavior that marked their lives at times.

There are exceptions, such as Abel, Enoch, Samuel and a few others about whom we would be hard pressed to find fault. Then there are the others, the majority in fact; whose lifestyles often looked more like a dirty movie than the biography of a Bible character. Abraham is a prime example. Others are equally as questionable by modern church standards.

Noah is listed as a person of great faith, yet the man was found lying in a drunken stupor no sooner than the ground was dry enough for him to fall down on after leaving the ark. In Genesis 8:20, he is seen building an altar shortly after he stepped out of the ark, but in 9:21 he is drunk and naked, apparently involved in some kind of disgusting situation about which Bible scholars have argued for centuries.

Study the lives of the heroes of faith mentioned in Hebrews 11 and take heart. There was Isaac. Read Genesis 26:6-9. What sin did he commit?

_____

Jacob is remembered until this day as a sneaky and conniving man for much of his lifetime.

Moses is mentioned in Hebrews 11. What did he do?
_____ (You can find the answer in Exodus 2:11-12.)

Samson and David are on the list. Do you remember what sins they both had in common?

_____

Hebrews 11:31 plainly refers to Rahab as "Rahab the _____."

If you were to erase the names of those mentioned in Hebrews 11 who had committed sins about which they would be ashamed, it would be a very short chapter. However, God chose not to erase their names when He inspired the writing of Scripture, but instead included them with full knowledge that we would see both their glory days and their gory days. It is almost as if there is a subliminal message contained in that list which says, "Don't think that God doesn't totally love you or that He can't use your life if you have sinned. Look at these people!"

As you end today's study, pray to your Father and admit to Him the things that have robbed you of peace and caused you to feel guilty to the point that it has held you back in your own grace walk. Then leave those things that have caused your guilt in His hands.

> *Don't think that God doesn't totally love you or that He can't use your life.*

# DAY TWO

## God Knows You Completely And Has Forgiven You

Yesterday we saw that God seems to be much more willing to put our past behind us than we often are. The people listed in Hebrews 11 were a contaminated lot, as far as being moral examples goes, but God put their past behind them and used their lives anyway. Know this – His love for you is no less. Consider the following person's experience and see if you can relate to his feelings.

"You don't understand, " Jess said to me one day. "I did my crime *after* I became a Christian. It's not like I didn't know what I was doing. I knew it was sin, but at the time I didn't care. I just knew I was tired of feeling poor. As the accountant, at first I just juggled the figures a little to get some extra spending money. Then, when I seemed to get away with it, I increased the amount I was embezzling. I thought my boss was oblivious to what I was doing. Then for the first time since I had worked there, he decided to have an outside audit done on the company. I had stolen tens of thousands of dollars before I was caught."

You probably haven't been to prison for any of the sins you have committed, but maybe you have had the same kind of nagging accusations in your mind that Jess expressed. In the modern church, we are quick to dismiss sins committed by a person before he became a Christian. Whether the sin was murder, immorality, divorce, drugs, stealing, you name it – it makes no difference. The common response is, "Yes, but that was *before* he became a Christian." The reasoning is absolutely correct. The sins a person committed before he became a believer have been forgiven. The cross has permanently and unchangeably removed them from us. God has separated them from us as and from Himself as far apart as the east is from the west. It's just like they never happened.

Christians have little problem understanding and accepting that fact, but what about the sins we have committed since then? We aren't so quick to forgive others or ourselves for the sins we have committed since becoming a Christian. The reason for this fact is that, because we live in a time dimension, many of us fail to understand the totality of God's eternal forgiveness for our sins.

## GOD'S RELATIONSHIP TO TIME

Albert Einstein once said, "The distinction between past, present, and future is only an illusion, however persistent." As human beings we live on that illusory time line. Our lifetime is a short segment of a continuum stretching from the creation of all things to the end of time. As time creatures, we experience events sequentially. However, Einstein was right about time being an illusion. Beyond the time continuum is God, who is not confined by it. He lives in the eternal present and sees all of history from beginning to end. He even sees beyond time into eternity past in one direction and eternity future in the other. Living beyond time, God views all events as happening simultaneously. Before you were born, God saw the time line of your life. Being omniscient, He knew everything you would ever think, do or say and yet still chose to save you from your sin and make you His own.

> *God lives in the eternal present and sees all of history from beginning to end.*

Let's go back to a couple of these heroes of the faith. Read Genesis 12:1. What did God tell Abraham to do?

_____

Did He know what Abraham would do in Egypt when He called him? Did God know that Noah would get falling-down-drunk as soon as he came

*Week Two*

off the ark when He told him to build it? Did He know in advance about the sins of Moses, Jacob, Samson, and David? Does God know everything about *everybody* in advance? Of course He does, yet He still chooses to call people to Himself.

God knew everything about you before you were even born. Living beyond the constraints of time, not only can He see everything in your life, He can also deal with it all at once. When you became a Christian, it wasn't just your past sins which were forgiven. *All* the sins of your lifetime were dealt with at the cross (see Colossians 2:13-14) and when Jesus bore them there, they were all still future as they related to time. When you became a believer, your sins were dealt with *in totality*. Every sin you have ever or will ever commit has been forgiven. It is just as if they never happened!

Do you believe that all your sins have been forgiven? If you do, write a statement saying so in the following space. Sign your name under the statement and date it.

_____

_____

_____

_____

When a Christian realizes that God's love is so generous that we have already been forgiven for every sin we will ever commit, that is a *huge* step toward being freed from a guilty conscious. Forgiveness of all our sins is a historical fact in the eternal realm.

Fill in the missing word in this verse, Romans 8:30:

*These whom he predestined, he also called; and these whom He called, He also justified; And these whom He justified, He also _____.*

Not only have we been justified, but also we have already been glorified with Christ in the heavens! How can this be true? It is because it has been done in the eternal realm. We simply haven't seen it in time yet, but make no mistake about it, it has already been done.

The realization of this fact frees us from condemnation over our past sins and obligation over future ones. We don't have to walk through life like we are in a minefield where we may step into temptation and have our faith be blown apart. Christians who know their identity in Christ aren't paranoid about sins and temptation. Our responsibility is to simply rest in Christ, allowing Him to love us and to live His life through us, dealing with sins and temptations as they approach us through the short time of our earth life.

God has forgiven your sins and forgotten them. It's that simple. Don't be hard on yourself, because God isn't! The sins you committed after you were born again are in the same category as the ones you committed before you became a Christian – forgiven and forgotten!

## HOW COULD GOD LOVE SOMEBODY LIKE ME?

"I do believe that God has forgiven all my sins," Wendy said. "But I'm still struggling about the sins that I don't seem to have victory over yet. I can't accept that He really loves me as much as He could, when I won't turn away from my sins. I'm trying to do better, but I keep failing. I know I must be a disappointment to God." Wendy's perspective is very common among Christians who focus on areas of their lives where they see inconsistency. She believed that somehow God would feel better toward her if she would clean up her act. Is it true that God's feelings toward us are affected by how we behave?

*Is it true that God's feelings toward us are affected by how we behave?*

One aspect of the good news of the gospel is that we can bring our weaknesses and sins to God through Christ and openly acknowledge them. We don't have to deny our sins. We don't have to make excuses about them. We don't even need to make promises about how we will try to do better. After all, many of us have learned that we *can't* do better even when we try. Legalism insists that we improve our behavior for God's sake, but grace gently encourages us to simply own it, and then lay it at the foot of the cross. When we see sins in our lifestyle, the best thing we can do with them is to *run* to our heavenly Father, lay them out before Him in all their ugliness, with the assurance that "God is to us, a God of deliverances" (Psalm 68:20).

*Week Two*

What are the areas of your life where you are vulnerable? Write a short prayer to your heavenly Father here, telling Him about them:

_____

_____

_____

_____

## YOUR FATHER WON'T LET YOU GO

When my grandson was a baby, I was holding him on my lap one day. I was laughing at him to see if I could get him to laugh. It worked. Every time I would laugh, Jonathan saw my delight in him and he laughed too. As we sat on the couch laughing together, I was filled with emotion and thought to myself, "It's amazing how much love I feel for him."

At that moment a thought came into my mind that I knew was the voice of God. "That's nothing compared to the love that I have for you." I was overwhelmed by the realization that my heavenly Father loves me infinitely greater than I could ever love my grandchildren or children.

> *Our heavenly Father loves us infinitely greater than we could ever love our grandchildren or children.*

As we continued to play together on the couch, I became increasingly aware that Jonathan had "sinned against me." It was a diaper problem, a serious one. Here I was holding him on my lap, showering him with attention and affection and he goes and does something like *that*! What do you suppose I did? I didn't throw him from my lap in anger, screaming, "Depart from me, you worker of iniquity!" Not at all. You see, I understand something about babies – they do that kind of thing. I wasn't pleased with his behavior, but what he did changed absolutely nothing between the two of us.

Jonathan eventually outgrew that habit and began to act responsibly in that area of life. As I thought about the incident shortly after it happened, I was reminded of our Father's patience and loving kindness toward us. He is always interacting in our lives with a divine determination to cause us to find pleasure in Him. Yet at the very same time, we sometimes sin against Him. We make a mess of things, despite His continuous commitment to cause all things to work together for our good.

When we sin against Him, does He cast us off? Absolutely not! "For He Himself knows our frame; He is mindful that we are but dust" (Psalm 103:14). What does that verse mean to you?

_____

_____

When Jonathan experienced his baby problem, his mood soon changed from happy to sad. He began to cry, instinctively knowing that he needed some sort of help from somebody bigger than himself. That is what happens in the lives of believers when we sin. We know that Somebody bigger who loves us will take care of our problem and deliver us from what we've gotten ourselves into at the moment. We just cry out to Him in dependence and anticipation and He does the rest.

Your Father knows you better than you know yourself. The things that have caused you to feel guilty have already been dealt with by His finished work on the cross. Remind yourself all through the day today that your sins have been forgiven and you have already been glorified with Christ in the eternal realm!

# DAY THREE

## Jesus Finished What He Started

So far you have seen from your study this week that you haven't messed up so badly in your life that God has set you aside and decided to look for somebody else who is better suited to be used by Him. (The people listed in Hebrews 11 should cause you to feel confident about that fact.) You have learned that every sin you have ever committed, both before and since you became a Christian, has been forgiven. The question you must now answer is, "How are you going to view your sins now?"

If God has forgiven every sin we will ever commit during our lifetime, what biblical option does that leave for us in regard to how we relate to sin? There is only one thing I can think of that is an appropriate response to the sins of our past – get over it! It is astounding to see the preoccupation that the modern church has with the subject of sin.

### DO YOU THINK LIKE A LEGALIST OR A GRACE-WALKER?

Legalism will cause us to stay focused on sins, but grace will enable us to redirect our focus away from our sins, past or present and place our full attention on Jesus Christ, who alone can cause us to say no to temptation. Make no mistake about it, when we are more absorbed in the consciousness of our sins than we are our forgiveness, we have become trapped in legalism. I want to prove that statement to you from the book of Hebrews.

In Hebrews 9, the Bible compares the Old Covenant of the Law (legalism) with the new covenant of grace, as each relates to the matter of sin.

The emphasis there is on how much better the New Covenant (Testament) is than the Old Covenant (Testament). One major aspect of the difference between the two has to do with how sins are regarded under each covenant.

Note how sins were dealt with under the Old Covenant:

*"...the priests are continually entering the outer tabernacle performing the divine worship, but into the second, only the high priest enters once a year, not without taking blood, which he offers for himself and for the sins of the people committed in ignorance" (9:6-7).*

How often did the priest have to go into the temple and offer sacrifices to deal with the matter of sins?

_____

Verse 9 says, "Accordingly both gifts and sacrifices are offered which cannot make the worshiper perfect in conscience." The *New Living Translation* says it this way: For the gifts and sacrifices that the priests offer are not able to cleanse the consciences of the people who bring them."

After the priests offered the sacrifices, did it cause the people who had sinned to have a clean conscience? _____

It is important to understand that the sacrifices under the Old Covenant didn't take away people's sins. It only covered them. Every year the high priest would have to go into the Holy of Holies to repeat the process, pushing everybody's sins forward in anticipation of the coming of Christ.

Read this passage in Hebrews 10:1-3, as translated in the *New Living Translation:*

> The old system in the law of Moses was only a shadow of the things to come, not the reality of the good things Christ has done for us. The sacrifices under the old system were repeated again and again, year after year, but they were never able to provide perfect cleansing for those who came to worship. If they could have provided perfect cleansing, the sacrifices would have stopped, for the worshipers would have

> *The sacrifices under the Old Covenant didn't take away people's sins.*

been purified once for all time, *and their feelings of guilt would have disappeared.* But just the opposite happened. Those yearly sacrifices reminded them of their sins year after year. (emphasis added)

Why did the feelings of guilt the people had about their past sins not disappear? It is because the sacrifice was not perfect. It was a band-aid job to cover their sins another year while they waited for the Great Physician to show up on planet earth. The sacrifices only covered the sins, it didn't take away them away. The people might have been okay for another year, but they knew what was "beneath the band-aid" and their consciences still bothered them about it.

> *The sacrifices only covered the sins, it didn't take away them away.*

What did the yearly sacrifices remind the people of every year?

_____

What happened inside them as a result of that reminder? (The answer is italicized in the text above.)

_____

What a wonderful day when Jesus Christ showed up here on earth! He came to take care of this whole sin issue, once and for all!

*"Under the Old Covenant, the priest stands before the altar day after day, offering sacrifices that can never take away sins. But our High Priest offered Himself to God as one sacrifice for sins, good for all time. Then he sat down at the place of highest honor at God's right hand"* (Hebrews 10:11-12 NLT).

The Old Covenant priest stood before the altar day by day, trying to offer enough sacrifices to take away sins. His role is comparable to being given a mop and told to go mop up the incoming tide at the beach. But Jesus didn't stand there, day after day, fighting a losing battle. He came. He offered Himself to God as a sacrifice for our sins and He sat down. Job completed. Done. Finished...forever.

*Journey into Intimacy*

## FINISHED MEANS FINISHED

One of the last things Jesus said on the cross was "It is *finished!*" The root of the word comes from the Greek word *teleo*, which means: to bring to a close, to finish, to end, passed, finished, to perform a last act which completes a process" (*Strong's Concordance*, Strong's Number 5055).

Why did Jesus go to the cross? To settle the matter of the debt we owe for our sins. When He said, "It is finished – passed – a closed matter," to what was He referring?

_____

Paul said in Colossians 2:14:

*He canceled the record that contained the charges against us. He took it and destroyed it by nailing it to Christ's cross. (NLT)*

The question you have to answer is, do you believe that Jesus Christ fully and completely dealt with every sin you would commit or not? Did He succeed or was He mistaken when He said, "It is finished?"

> *Do you believe that Jesus Christ fully and completely dealt with every sin you would commit or not?*

If He intended that we should still wallow in guilt about our sins, then it wasn't totally finished, was it? Under the old covenant, the work of the high priest was never finished. There was the ongoing need to go back into the holy of holies and offer up the sacrifice again and again. Hebrews 10:3 said that if what the priest did at the altar on behalf of the people had finished the job "their feelings of guilt would have disappeared."

When Jesus came, He finished dealing with our sins. Look up Hebrews 1:3 in your own Bible. Fill in the blanks:

*When He had made purification of sins, He _____ at the right hand of the Majesty on high.*

Why did He do that?

_____

*Week Two*

Hebrews 10:12 says, "having offered one sacrifice for sins for all time, he sat down at the right hand of God." Why? Because there was nothing left to do regarding our sins. He dealt with our guilt and then sat down.

Under the old covenant of law, there could be no guilt-free conscience, but you don't live under that covenant. Jesus Christ did what the animal sacrifices of the Old Testament could never do – He took your sins away. The blood of Christ doesn't cover them. They have been removed and you have been *justified*. You may remember the meaning of that word as being *Just-if-I* never sinned! You have a clean slate in heaven now! (Remember Colossians 2:14?) So, if you have a clean record in heaven, there is no reason at all for you not to have a clean conscience on earth.

Your conscience may bother you over past sins, but John said that if your heart condemns you, remember that God is greater than your heart and He knows all things.(See 1 John 3:20) He knows that your sins have been totally forgiven. Do you know that? Do you believe it?

John goes on to say that if you live your life without feeling condemned by a guilty conscience, it will give you tremendous confidence in your grace walk. (See 1 John 3:21) A guilty conscience is seriously debilitating to your Christian walk, but a clean conscience sets you free to live boldly!

As you end today's study, review the verses you have read and apply them to your own life. Then pray and thank your heavenly Father that Jesus finished what He came to do and that your sins really are gone, no matter how you might have felt about it in the past.

# Jesus Christ Has
# Put Away Our Sins Forever

*Y*esterday we discussed that Jesus Christ fully accomplished what He came to do about our sins. Although the duty of the Old Testament priest was never complete, Jesus declared that the job was finished as a result of His sacrifice.

The Apostle Paul wrote in Romans that we are now "dead to sin" (Romans 6:11) and have no relationship to it anymore. (See Romans 6:7) By His finished work at the cross, Christ dealt with both our old sin nature and with the specific sins that we will commit during our lifetime.

This week our study has been about the sins we commit which have caused us to have a guilty conscience. Why shouldn't you feel guilty about sins you have committed anymore? Because God has forgiven them – it's that simple. If God says it is a closed matter, it is done.

## PUTTING AWAY SIN

To suggest that we set aside the guilt for our sins seems wrong to the legalistic mind. Some might suggest that this kind of approach is to be "soft on sin," but nothing could be further from the truth. In fact, the converse is true. To suggest that what Jesus did on the cross isn't sufficient to adequately deal with our guilt concerning sin is to be *soft on grace*! In other words, to insist that we still carry around guilt over our sins is an attempt to weaken the effectiveness of the finished work of Christ! When Jesus said it was finished, He meant it.

Today, our focus will be on how we are to regard the sins in our lives. Let's begin with a powerful statement about what Christ has done with our sins. Consider the meaning of Hebrews 9:26:

*...but now once at the consummation of the ages He has been manifested to put away sin by the sacrifice of Himself.*

What did Jesus do with sin? _____

The Bible says that Jesus came "to put away sin by the sacrifice of Himself." What Jesus came to *put away*, many modern Christians enjoy discussing, studying, arguing about, rebuking, renouncing, outlining, participating in, and being obsessed with most of the time. If Jesus came to put it away, why do we keep trying to take it back out?

> *Do you believe that Jesus Christ fully and completely dealt with every sin you would commit or not?*

It isn't possible for you to have a guilty conscience without taking out something that Jesus Christ came to put away. The obsession many Christians have with sin fuels a guilty conscience about their past and stimulates sin in their daily walk. Paul wrote, "the mind set on the flesh is death, but the mind set on the Spirit is life and peace" (Romans 8:6).

The fastest track to kill your joy and confidence about your Christian life is to spend your time thinking about the sins of the flesh. Jesus put that away, so why would we want to take it back out again?

## GUILTY FEELINGS ABOUT WHAT WE HAVEN'T DONE

The fact that believers now possess the righteous nature of Jesus Christ (see Romans 5:17,19) doesn't do away with the reality that we still must contend with the power of the indwelling sin that exists in our bodies. (See Romans 7:23) A grace walk *enables* us to experience victory over temptation, but it doesn't eliminate the possibility for sin.

In my book, *Grace Walk*, I explained how I felt guilty about the things I hadn't done that I believed must be done in order to be a good Christian.

*Journey into Intimacy*

*I lived many years of my Christian life trapped in what I call the motivation-condemnation-rededication cycle. From the earliest years of my Christian life I had a mental picture of what I thought I should be. But in my mind there was always a wide gap between where I ought to be and where I was.*

*Sometimes when I was especially motivated I would feel that the gap had narrowed a little. When I was winning people to Christ or spending a lot of time praying and studying the Bible, I felt that I might actually one day be able to achieve my goal of being a victorious Christian. But inevitably the time would come when my motivation level would diminish and my fury and fire would die down. That always led to a sense of condemnation. Even when I had really done nothing wrong to cause the condemnation, I would often feel guilty for not doing all the things that I believed I should be doing. The devil would have a field day with me during this phase.*

*Sometimes I would become spiritually indifferent. I often wondered if I would ever be consistent in my Christian life. I would wallow in my misery until I couldn't stand it anymore, then would finally rededicate myself to God, confessing my sins and spiritual slothfulness. I would pray, and with genuine contempt for my inconsistency, would ask God to help me to be more consistent. I would promise to read my Bible more, pray more, win more souls, whatever I thought it took to get back on course. I resolved to try harder than ever to live for God. Yet no matter how hard I tried, I never experienced real peace about my Christian life.*

> The finished work of Christ is sufficient to free us from guilt.

For the most part, the things I felt guilty about were not sins of commission, but sins of omission. It was what I *hadn't done* that made me feel guilty. Can you relate? The fact is that not only is the finished work of Christ sufficient to free us from guilt about the things we've done, but also about our failures in the areas where we haven't done what we believed we should do.

## GUILTY FEELINGS ABOUT WHAT WE HAVE DONE

Here is the other side of the coin. I received an email from Stephen, whose mother committed suicide when he was ten years old. Early in life he turned to pornography in an attempt to ease his pain. He describes,

By the time I was 11 years old, I had become heavily involved in pornography as an attempt to find relief from the pain of my mother's death. But I didn't really see it as really that bad. "They're just pictures," I would think to myself.

When I was in high school, a couple of my buddies explained the gospel to me, and for the first time in my life I saw that I was a sinner and I needed a Savior. I received Jesus and made a commitment to live for God and obey Him in every area of my life. I sincerely tried to live right, but I was hooked on pornography and I couldn't will myself to stop. I tried everything. I prayed, fasted, and memorized all the Scripture that have to do with sexual sin, went to deliverance services, paid my tithes (as if I could buy my freedom), witnessed to as many friends as I could, blocked internet porn and 1-900 sex lines. These are just a few of the things I did, but when it was all said and done, I was still in bondage.

I had decided to commit suicide when a friend of mine suggested I read your book, Grace Walk. As God began to teach me who I am in Christ, it began to sink in that the only answer is Christ and the cross. I finally saw it. It is only through the cross that I am free. I was and am elated. Thank God, the answer to my problem was not more religious rules (which only leads to condemnation and death), but instead it is simply God's grace through Jesus Christ.

> *God loves you so much that He has already done everything necessary for you to walk in freedom continuously.*

"My guilty conscience was caused primarily by believing I wasn't doing all that I should be doing." Here was somebody whose chronic sense of guilt was because of something wrong he was doing. Is there a sin in your lifestyle from which you cannot seem to break free? If so, you probably have to battle a guilty conscience much of the time. Legalism offers a thousand answers for things you can *do* to find freedom, but in reality God loves you so much that He has already done everything necessary for you to walk in freedom continuously.

The key to freedom is the indwelling life of Jesus Christ. If we are to agree with the finished work of Christ and put away sin, we must understand that He alone is our victory. We can never overcome the sins that cause us to feel guilty by our own determination.

Stephen's guilty conscience almost drove him to the point of suicide. Thankfully, he discovered that the key to freedom had been in his possession since the day he received Christ. God loves us so much that He *put away* sin from us. You have the option to act as if it hasn't been put away, but, in Jesus Christ, victory over sin is ours if we simply appropriate it by faith. Is there a besetting sin in your life? Put it away and get over it!

> On a scale of one to ten, with ten meaning that you are consumed with a guilty conscience, what level of guilt has characterized your mind for most of your Christian life? _____

> What number would you assign to the intensity of a guilty conscience at this very moment? _____

> Scoring on this system from one to ten, what number would reflect the level of guilt you have in God's eyes? _____

Is there a discrepancy between the number you assigned yourself and the level of guilt that God sees in you? I hope you realize that, from God's perspective, your level of guilt is *zero*. That should have been your answer to the last question.

Jesus came to put away everything that would have raised your guilt level above a zero. Did He succeed? The important issue in facing your own guilty conscience is to realize that you aren't a victim. You have a God-given ability to choose to say no to a guilty conscience until you realize freedom over it in your daily walk.

> *You have a God-given ability to choose to say no to a guilty conscience.*

Paul said in Romans 12:2, "Do not be conformed to this world, but be transformed through the renewing of your mind." Make no mistake about it, any nagging sense of guilt that a Christian may have is a "mind problem." The cause is that our thoughts aren't in line with what God's Word says about the matter.

As you end today's study, will you be honest with your Father about any nagging sense of guilt you may have? Ask Him to renew your mind to the truth that your sins have been forgiven and that it is a closed matter now. Jesus put away your sins by sacrificing Himself. Will you resolve to leave them where He put them, which is under His grace?

*Dear Father,*

_____

_____

_____

_____

_____

_____

*Amen*

# Walking In The Truth Of Forgiveness

*Y*our study this week has been for the purpose of teaching you to leave your guilty conscience at home as you continue on your journey into intimacy with God. Have you taken that step of faith and determined, by God's grace, to renounce a guilty conscience? To fail to do so is to unnecessarily weigh ourselves down with a lot of baggage that will only serve to slow us down spiritually.

The burden of a guilty conscience is a disease among Christians. It is amazing to see how many Christians are drawn toward self-condemnation. There is a sad irony in the lifestyle of a believer who nurses a guilty conscience. The irony is that he is actually committing a sin by wallowing in guilt about his sin.

An attitude of self-condemnation is nothing less than an assault on the finished work of Christ by seeking to punish ourselves for our own sins. To punish ourselves by self-loathing is to imply that when Jesus declared, "It is finished," He was wrong. "There is still something left for me to do – detest myself," this attitude of unbelief insists.

Self-condemnation is a sacrament to the Christian legalist. It is one way that he seeks to pay for his sins. His rationale may be conscious or unconscious, but it suggests that if he is sorry enough; if he feels badly enough;

if he beats himself up enough, and offers up the sacrifice of genuine self contempt, *then* God will forgive him.

While his demeanor appears to be one of contrition, in reality his attitude demonstrates the worst kind of pride, which is both gaudy and despicable. He actually thinks that there is something *he* can do to bring on forgiveness. His self centered, pay-your-own-way-with-the-currency-of-guilt, attitude is an affront to the finished work of Jesus Christ.

He talks a talk that sounds like a godly man to many, but his self-absorbed loathing of himself betrays a brazen and adulterous affair with the law. He may have died to the law so that he could be joined to Jesus Christ, (see Romans 7:4) but his insistence on wallowing in the bed of self-judgment with the law suggests a religious hedonism that brings him great pleasure in the darkest places of his flesh.

Jesus came to "put away sin by the sacrifice of *Himself*," says the Bible. If He didn't succeed at that, then our hopes are all in vain. If He did succeed, then any attempt to add another word to what the cross has spoken by allowing ourselves to accept self-condemnation is an attempt to dilute, and thus negate, its power. Can this be called anything less than *sin*?

## RENEWING OUR MINDS TO GOD'S TRUTH

Have you sinned against God by allowing yourself to entertain self-condemnation about your sins, past or present? Renounce your sin and run into the loving arms of your heavenly Father, giving up both your sins and your self-condemnation to Him. Lay it all at His feet and allow Him to simply love you. Judgment day for you is finished. It was over at the cross when Jesus declared it to be so. God has nothing to say to you now other than words of love and acceptance. Don't struggle against Him, but simply accept the truth.

*Judgment day for you is finished.*

Write a short prayer here, turning away from self-condemnation:

_____

_____

Allow the following verses to renew your mind to the truth about what God has done in regard to your sins. Use your Bible and fill in the blanks:

**Micah 7:19** He will again have compassion on us; He will tread our iniquities underfoot. Yes,

You will _____.

**Psalm 103:12** As far as the east is from the west, So far has He

_____.

**Isaiah 43:25** I, even I, am the One who wipes out your transgressions for my own sake, and I will not _____.

**Colossians 2:13** He made you alive together with Him, having forgiven us _____ our transgressions.

**Hebrews 8:12** For I will be merciful to their iniquities, and I will _____ no more.

**1 Peter 2:24** He Himself bore our sins in His body on the cross, so that we might die to sin and live to righteousness; for by His wounds _____.

**1 John 2:12** I am writing to you, little children, because _____ for His name's sake.

**1 John 3:5** You know that He appeared to _____; and in Him there is no sin.

**Revelation 1:5** And from Jesus Christ, the faithful witness, the firstborn of the dead, and the ruler of the kings of the earth. To Him who loves us and _____ by His blood.

Did you note the two steps necessary in overcoming a guilty conscience? They are *renounce* and *renew*. We renounce the lie that we still bear guilt before God and we renew our minds with the truth of God's Word that our sins have been dealt with in totality and that we no longer have any relationship to them whatsoever.

Your sin is gone. It is forgiven and forgotten. The cross of Jesus Christ has dealt with all your past, present and future sins. There is nothing to stand in your way now that prevents a continuous intimate, loving relationship to God. The truth is that you are beautiful because by your co-crucifixion with Christ, everything that wasn't beautiful was taken away from you.

*Week Two*

You are a new creation now (see 2 Corinthians 5:17) and all the old things that could have caused you guilt and anxiety are forever gone. The books have been reconciled on your sins, with an eternal declaration that they have been paid in full. God will never even so much as question you about them. (See Hebrews 9:28) It's time now for you to put them away from you once and for all. Don't waste your energy on something that God has forgotten. Instead, choose to simply enjoy Him, completely free from every trace of guilt and condemnation.

> *Don't waste your energy on something that God has forgotten.*

As your study this week comes to a close, it is important to identify this mile marker in your journey into a deeper intimacy with God. Have you settled this matter of a guilty conscience this week? You may still experience feelings of guilt and accusing thoughts at times, but when they arise remember that you aren't a helpless victim to them. Affirm the truth of God's Word that your sins have been forgiven and then act that way.

Your feelings may not instantly change, but over a period of time as you continue to affirm God's truth in your life you will find increasing freedom. After all, that's what truth does in our lives. John 8:32 says that, "you will know the truth, and the truth will make you free." So cling to the truth! As you find increasing healing in your emotions and mind concerning your sins, you will experience a growing sense of intimacy with your Father.

# DON'T WORRY ABOUT MAKING MISTAKES

## God Is In Charge

*I* once read a statement by the famous president of a Bible college in which he said that if he had his whole life to do over again, he wouldn't change one thing he had done. I found his statement to be puzzling. How could any man say that and mean it? Was every decision he made the perfect one? I can't speak for his track record, but I know that I've done some dumb things in my life, things I definitely would do differently if I had them to do over again.

Are there things you've done in your life that you would change if you could? I don't mean sins you have committed. I'm referring to choices that you made which would be different if you knew then what you know now.

I remember a time shortly after I was married that I decided that I was being called to New York City to work with an organization that ministered to the street people. I convinced my eighteen-year-old bride, Melanie, that this was our divine calling, and then, as an "act of faith," I proceeded to sell every single item we owned, with the exception of our bed and refrigerator (the two most important home furnishings for a newlywed). A few months later, when the New York ministry declined my offer to come and help, we found ourselves living in an almost empty house for quite some time.

I'm not alone in being one who made a foolish decision, am I? What is one decision you have made in your life that you would do differently if you could start over again?

*Week Three*

My bright idea of moving to New York City on a whim was only one of my blunders in life. I won't list them all, lest you come to believe I'm a complete idiot. I share this one from my early adult life to illustrate the point that sincere Christians can make foolish decisions sometimes. Unlike my decision to move to New York, some of our impulsive decisions actually materialize. We act on them, and then later wonder if we can ever be all that we could have been had we not made those foolish choices.

> *Sincere Christians can make foolish decisions sometimes.*

Ruth approached me after I spoke at her church one day and said, "I have never felt the kind of closeness to God that I want. I believe the reason is because of my marriage. I married my husband at an early age. I had hardly even dated anybody else. Our relationship has been rocky for the whole twenty years we've been married. I had planned to be a missionary before I met him. I've sometimes wondered if my decision to marry was an impulsive mistake made by a young girl who really was experiencing nothing more than being in love with love. I have always felt that God was disappointed with me for not going on to be a missionary."

## THE EFFECT OF MISTAKES IN LIFE

Ruth believed that she had made a choice that would prevent her from experiencing God's best for her as long as she lives. It's not that she chose to sin against God. She believes it was an honest mistake she made, but thinks that her choice will somehow negatively affect her so that now she will always have to settle for God's second best and spend the rest of her life wondering what might have been.

This kind of attitude is a subtle trap of the enemy that can keep the Christian from experiencing deep intimacy with God. After all, how can one have a close, loving, and transparent relationship to somebody if we know that person can't forget the fact that we've made a mistake that can never be undone, a mistake that caused him to have to completely change the original plans *he* had.

Intimacy with God is challenging if you believe that you've made an irrevocable mistake that has brought His disapproval. When we've made choices that we believe have fouled things up, it's hard to really believe that God will give us the very best we might have had otherwise. We sometimes tend to think that even though He will bless us, it won't be as good as it might have been. Even though we may believe it is our own fault, this kind of attitude will interfere with how we perceive God charting our life course.

You may have made decisions that you believe might have messed up the way your life *could* have been if you had made wiser choices. There is good news that can set you free from that kind of damaging perspective. The news is that *God's love is bigger than your mistakes!* No mistake you have ever made or ever could make will cause your life to jump track.

During your study this week, you are going to see that we aren't big enough to short-circuit God's plan for our lives. There is no way that you have done something that has forced you to now have to accept "God's second best" for your life. You're going to see through our study this week that God has no second best. "Plan B" just isn't in His frame of reference.

You belong to God and it is His responsibility, not yours, to insure that you stay the course. That fact is inherent to the very meaning of the word *grace*, which suggests it's all up to Him, not you. You may make apparent detours in life, but God's love for you is great enough that He won't allow you to veer off His assigned path and wander out of His will for your life.

> *No mistake you have ever made or ever could make will cause your life to jump track.*

## A Sovereign God

The Psalmist said that, "The Lord has established His throne in the heavens; And His sovereignty rules over all" (Psalm 103:19). This world doesn't exist in a cosmic setting in which events happen by chance. Everything in existence functions under the superintending guidance of a sovereign God. On the grand scale, "By Him all things were created, in the heavens and on earth, visible and invisible, whether [it is] thrones or dominions or rulers or authorities – all things have been created through Him and for Him (Colossians 1:16).

God is a big God who has everything under control. The stars don't hang there in the sky on nothingness. They are held there by the omnipotent

will of a sovereign God. The tide on the beach doesn't coincidently stop at its boundaries and return to the sea. It is ordered back by divine design. The earth doesn't keep spinning on its axis under its own momentum. God designed it that way.

However, this same God who attends to the majestic details of the universe also gives meticulous attention to the minutia of life. Consider what Jesus said in Matthew 10:29-30:

> *Are not two sparrows sold for a cent? And yet not one of them will fall to the ground apart from your Father. But the very hairs of your head are all numbered.*

The Bible says that He has the hairs of your head numbered. That's serious attention to detail!

Personalize the verse by describing in your own words what relevance it has to do with your life and specific circumstances:

_____

_____

_____

_____

Our God is Lord of both the macroscopic and the microscopic. Nothing is too big or too small to be beyond His direct control. He knows and cares about every detail of your life, regardless of how great or how small it may seem to you.

Considering that man is God's crowning touch in creation and that Christians in particular are His divine workmanship (see Ephesians 2:10), don't think for a minute that God isn't up close and personal in the affairs of your life. He is intricately interested in your daily routine. He guards and guides you as you move through life.

Proverbs 5:21 says, "For the ways of a man are before the eyes of the Lord, And He watches all his paths." The word "watches" in that verse doesn't simply mean that He happens to notice. It means that He looks intensely at you, taking careful note of your actions. The idea is that your loving Father comes alongside you, with His face inches away from yours, carefully examining, scrutinizing, analyzing every move you make. Not only does God watch your actions, but He even ponders your attitudes and the motivation that cause you to do the things you do. (See Proverbs 21:2) God has His eye on you and always has.

> *God has His eye on you and always has.*

As you end today's study, write a personal declaration of your belief in the sovereignty of God. In your own words, acknowledge that He has always been and always will be in complete charge of your life. You don't have to understand the "whys" of your own circumstances. Right now, you just need to settle the fact and embrace the truth that God is in charge and that nothing that has ever happened or ever will happen in your life occurs beyond His knowledge and control.

## MY DECLARATION OF GOD'S SOVEREIGNTY IN MY LIFE

_____

_____

_____

_____

_____

This I believe in spite of any circumstantial evidence to the contrary,

Signed _____

## DAY TWO

# God Is Bigger Than Our Mistakes

An important factor in moving further in our journey into intimacy with God is to learn to rest in the fact that He is in charge, not us. That was the focus of your study yesterday. Your Father loves you and He will be sure that nothing you do will ever cause you to permanently jump track. Don't think for a minute that mistakes you have made can disqualify you from His blessings and love.

Today, we will further examine the reality that no wrong choice you could ever make is enough to put you on the sidelines of life. Grace doesn't work that way and your Father is a God of grace. He has great plans for you.

There is not one person who is *continuously* on my mind, but you are never out of God's conscious thought or away from His immediate attention. He has been obsessed with you for all eternity and can't take His mind off you. He is so in love with you that He has committed all the resources at His disposal (which are considerable) to your wellbeing. God has never glanced away from you for a moment, so that in that moment you did something He didn't expect. He has set you right in front of His face and will keep you there forever. (See Psalm 41:12) David, the Psalmist said, "You scrutinize my path" (Psalm 139:3).

Have you ever felt like God was nowhere to be found at a time in your life when you really needed Him? Are there decisions you made that, once you saw the results, you wondered why He allowed you to make those choices? The fact is that if you were to combine the negative consequences of every regrettable decision made in your whole lifetime, the weight of those consequences would be nothing compared to the God-sized Sovereignty that rules over the affairs of your life.

The enemy of your soul wants you to believe the lie that suggests that you have made choices that now negatively affect how God relates to you or limits the extent to which He can use your life for His glory. That just isn't so. The One who started His work in you will be the One who completes it. (See Philippians 1:6)

Daniel the prophet wrote:

*All the inhabitants of the earth are accounted as nothing, But He does according to His will in the host of heaven and {among} the inhabitants of the earth, And no one can ward off His hand or say to Him, What have you done? (4:35)*

Rewrite that verse in your own words:

_____

_____

_____

_____

I would paraphrase the verse to say: "People in this world aren't the center of everything. God is and He does exactly what He wants to do, both in heaven and on the earth. Nobody can reach out and stop His hand from doing what He wants to do and nobody can ask Him, "What do you think you're doing?"

The fact is that you and I aren't big enough to foul up God's plans. Let's not flatter ourselves. *Our* decisions causing God to fail to get His way? Common sense (and the Bible) tells us better than that!

What about sins we have committed? Did God "will" those to happen? Trying to wrap our minds around that question can almost make you dizzy!

*Week Three*

Let me ask you a question: Did God put it into the hearts of the men who crucified Jesus to commit that offense? Of course not. God can't tempt men to do evil. (See James 1:13)

On the other hand, was it God's intent from the foundation of the world that Jesus should be crucified to save us from our sin? Yes, it was. (See Acts 2:23; 1 Peter 1:19-20)

In the mind of our Sovereign God, there is perfect balance between those two aspects of the crucifixion.

## THE WORST DECISION EVER MADE BY MAN

Wouldn't you agree that when wicked men crucified the Son of God, that could be considered the worst sin committed in human history? However, despite the choice they made to crucify Jesus, God's purpose was not thwarted. Not in the least. In fact, His Sovereignty overwhelmed their wickedness and the crucifixion of Jesus Christ became the hinge upon which the door of salvation swung wide open.

> *The crucifixion of Jesus Christ became the hinge upon which the door of salvation swung wide open.*

Your wrong choice may have been more than what would be considered a simple mistake. It might have been a deliberate sin, but even if it was, God is bigger still. He doesn't fret over what we have or haven't done. His grace takes care of everything.

If God sovereignly worked the worst sin ever committed into His overall plan, do you really think you can make a wrong choice (whether it was a deliberate sin or simply an honest mistake) that can cause Him to have to step back and ask Himself what He is going to do now? Don't be fooled by that lie – you can't.

Before I understood this truth, one time I was scolding myself for a wrong choice I had made. "Because of my own foolishness, now God can't do the thing it was obvious He had planned!" I thought as I considered the situation at hand. At that moment, a thought popped into my head and said, "Don't kid yourself. You're not that strong." I think I know whose voice that was, don't you? God will do what God wants to do and we flatter ourselves when we think that we are big enough to stop it.

If God isn't in charge of everything, then how can we know He is in charge of anything? Timothy said that He is the "Only Potentate, the King of kings, and Lord of lords" (1 Timothy 6:15.) That's a clear explanation of the fact that He is the One in charge. He asks nobody's permission or advice for anything. He does what He wants and doesn't have to explain His reasoning to us.

There is much about God's sovereignty I don't understand – why He allows some things and why He prevents others. With no disrespectful irreverence intended, I'll admit that if I were in charge, I would often do things differently, but I'm not in charge. He is. We will never fully understand His unseen motives and methods.

There are things about God's sovereignty that none of us understand. If you could ask God a few questions about why He has allowed certain things in your life to happen or why He hasn't allowed particular things, what would you ask Him?

> *We will never fully understand His unseen motives and methods.*

_____

_____

_____

_____

Have you asked Him about these things? If not, ask Him now in prayer. Maybe He will give you answers immediately, maybe later in life, or maybe after you get to heaven. You will be given answers to your questions sooner or later, assuming you continue to care about the answers. You can count on it.

There are things we will not understand in this life about why God allowed certain things to happen in our lives as a result of things we have done. If we were able to completely understand God and His ways, our minds could contain Him and God can't be contained. God is God and we aren't. It's that simple.

Contemporary religion generally presents a God who is forced to submit to modern rationale, values, and predictable patterns of behavior. It markets a manageable God, offering the commodity of a comfortable, devotional experience – warm fuzzies on demand. On the other hand, the God of the Christian isn't like that. Our God is out of control, appearing on the scene at times displaying wild passion for those He loves and at other times appearing to have gone on a permanent vacation when we need Him most. Regardless of how hard we may try, we simply cannot figure Him out.

Trusting in the loving sovereignty of God becomes the natural response to an understanding of His heart toward those who are in Christ. Because you are *in Him*, He has all the bases of your life covered, regardless of what decisions you have already made or are still yet to make. You are *in Christ* and that fact makes all the difference in life. If the fundamental message of Scripture were to be reduced to two simple words, they would be, "in Christ," a phrase used 77 times in the New Testament.

> *You are in Christ and that fact makes all the difference in life.*

Contemporary teaching on Christianity often focuses on Christ being in *our* lives, but the emphasis of the New Testament is that we have entered into *His* life. "In Him we live and move and exist," wrote Luke. (See Acts 17:28) By the cross, God has put to death the old life we had (See Galatians 2:20; Romans 6:1-7; Colossians 3:3) and has now given us the very life of Jesus Christ to be our own.

The fact that we are now joined in union with Him gives us more than good coverage in terms of the mistakes we make in life. You have Deity living inside you! Not only that, but He loves you and has committed Himself to you for all eternity. Can you see how that if you really believe this, it will move you miles further down the road toward intimacy with God?

As you complete your study today, identify the questions you asked your Father earlier in today's study about the things you don't understand. Now, in prayer, place them in His hands and tell Him that you will wait for Him to give you answers. In the meantime, you will trust Him no matter what happens.

## Loving Arms Carry You

Through your studies this week, are you sensing the importance of understanding how mistakes are swallowed up by the awesome grace of God? To see our mistakes through the lens of His grace puts them in their proper perspective. Knowing that He is in charge and that His grace is bigger than the wrong choices we make becomes a gateway into intimacy with Him.

Your Father loves you so much that He has brought you to Himself, where you will stay in Christ for all eternity. Your choices do not keep you there. It's His decision. Through His grace, we have come home to rest in Him. If we are indeed "in Him," then everything is going to be okay. Mistakes we have made can't take away our security because our security doesn't rest in our circumstances, but in the God we love and Who loves us.

When Moses announced God's blessing on the tribes of Israel by promising to bring them into His place of rest, He gave the people an encouraging word that can foster a sense of intimate trust in God even today. He told them that, "the eternal God is a dwelling place, and underneath are the everlasting arms" (Deuteronomy 33:27).

Christians are in Christ, *and*, says the Bible, *underneath are the everlasting arms.* Do you know what it means to have God's everlasting arms underneath you? Whenever I read this verse, I associate this promise with a memory from my childhood.

## LEARNING TO RELAX

I remember when I learned to swim, as a child. It was in a Sunday School class party and everybody there seemed to know how to swim, except me. My teacher, noticing that I was in the shallow end of the pool, asked, "Steve, can't you swim?" "No," I answered embarrassingly. "Do you want me to teach you?" he asked. I agreed and he began his instruction. "The first thing you need to know," he said, "is that you don't have to be afraid of sinking and drowning. If you relax, your body *will* float. Just try lying on your back and relaxing in the water."

I lay back in the water, attempting to do what he had told me. However, every time I would lie back, I would feel my head sinking into the water, and the moment water filled my ears, I would lift my head. Then I would begin to sink. "Don't lift your head," my teacher encouraged me. "Just relax and let your ears go underwater. You won't sink." Again I would try to take his advice, but when I felt the water rising above my ears toward my face, I would rise up and again begin to sink.

Finally he came over toward me and said, "Lie back *in my arms* and I will hold you on top of the water so that you cannot sink." I began to lie back and, true to his word, I felt his arms underneath me, holding me up. As he held me there and I felt the support of his arms, I began to relax a little. After a short time, I was comfortable. Finally, he said to me, "Okay, now I'm going to move my arms from your back so that you won't feel me touching you, but *they will still be beneath you*, so that I will catch you if you start to sink. Do you trust me?" he asked. I expressed that I did trust him and he did exactly what he said. For the first time in my life, I floated on the water. I felt no fear because I knew that underneath me were his arms. I knew that I had his guarantee that he would not let me sink.

Have there been times in your life when decisions you have made caused you to say to yourself, "Oh no, I'm sunk now?" What is one of those occasions that come to mind?

_____

I have been at places like that in my life many times. There were times I wondered how I would survive my circumstances. I felt certain that disaster was imminent. My assessment always proved to be wrong. Whether I felt it or not, underneath me were God's everlasting arms keeping me from sinking. The same is true of your life. You are where you are today because God has upheld you by His arms. The arms of God provide a lifetime guarantee that He will take care of the details of our lives, ensuring that we won't make choices that cause us to sink to a place where He doesn't want us to be. You can relax and enjoy the water because God has you in His arms.

Maybe your situation didn't have the resolution you had hoped for, but know this for sure – your Father has held you up in every situation you have ever faced. Just because you may have been disappointed with the outcome of your circumstances at times doesn't mean He forgot you. He has held you and His arms will uphold you forever.

## THE ARMS OF GOD

What kind of arms does God have? The Bible speaks often about His arms and gives us some insight into the Person in whom we are placing our trust. Consider these biblical descriptions of the arm of God:

> *You are where you are today because God has upheld you by His arms.*

### God has outstretched arms

This is the most common description of God's arm used in Scripture. To say that the arm of God is outstretched is to suggest that God is not passive about the affairs of our lives, but is actively involved orchestrating events for our good and His glory. The majority of times that the arm of God is described in Scripture as being stretched out is when He works on behalf of those whom He loves to rescue them from circumstances that could potentially destroy them.

What do the following verses say that God did for His people with an outstretched arm?

Exodus 6:6 _____

Deuteronomy 5:15 _____

Psalm 136:10-12 _____

*Week Three*

These verses make it clear that God delivers His people from hard circumstances with and outstretched arm. The outstretched arm of God reveals His power. He is capable of freeing us from any disaster we face in life, even if we are in that place because of our own choices.

> *God is capable of freeing us from any disaster we face in life.*

One day, when we get to heaven, we will see the many times not recognized in this world when the arm of God reached out into our circumstances to rescue us from what would have been certain disaster. The Psalmist often wrote songs honoring God for the many times He had delivered him from trying circumstances. Have you ever paused to identify the many known times when God did the same for you?

Ask the Lord to show you the many times He has rescued you from disaster. You may be surprised by the swelling sense of joy and gratitude you feel as God reveals how often He has acted on your behalf. This simple exercise may cause you to *feel* a sense of God's loving concern like you have seldom experienced.

**I remember God delivering me when:**

_____

_____

_____

_____

### God has strong arms

Reflecting upon the frequent times God had delivered Israel, David wrote, "You have a strong arm [and] your hand is mighty!" (Psalm 89:13-14) Well-meaning people often die trying to save others who are drowning. It isn't that their intention isn't good. They simply lack the strength to intervene and pull the person in distress from the water. Consequently, they both drown. Our God has the ever-present knowledge of our circumstances to know when we have gotten in over our heads; He has the loving desire to rescue us, and the strength to do exactly that!

Have your decisions brought you to the place where you don't think you're going to survive the circumstances? Take courage by knowing that the One who loves you has the muscle to deliver you! When the Apostle Peter once found himself in water over his head, the Bible says that, "beginning to sink, he cried, saying, 'Lord, save me!' and *immediately* the Lord stretched out his hand and took hold of him" (Matthew 14:30-31, emphasis added). In the days since then, the compassion of Jesus for those He loves hasn't been exhausted.

The One who ponders your every move always stands ready to respond to *your* cry. He could never stand by and watch you drown in a sea of wrong decisions, despite the fact that you may feel otherwise at times. You can trust that God's strong arm is always reaching out on your behalf.

### God has bare arms

Isaiah said that "The Lord has comforted His people... He has bared His holy arm" (Isaiah 52:9-10). God's involvement in your life is not casual. The reason His arm is bare is because He has rolled up His sleeves to go to work in your circumstances. Through the eyes of faith, see this all power-ful God – the One who spoke the world into existence; the One who with a word will destroy Satan; the One by whom all things in this world exist – see *that* God working hard on your behalf!

> *You can trust that God's strong arm is always reaching out on your behalf.*

Don't think for a minute that foolish choices you may have made can overrule the plans divinely devised by this bare-armed God who stretches out His strong arm into your circumstances to work out His purposes. While it is true that there is an enemy who would ruin the perfect plan God has for our lives, God *will not* allow it. As Martin Luther wrote in 1529:

*And though this world, with devils filled, should threaten to undo us,*
*We will not fear, for God hath willed His truth to triumph through us:*
*The Prince of Darkness grim, we tremble not for him;*
*His rage we can endure, for lo, his doom is sure,*
*One little word shall fell him.*

*Week Three*

If you want to go forward in your journey into intimacy with God through Jesus Christ, it is important to know and believe the truth concerning God's loving care in your life. He has carried you in His arms all along. You may still have questions that begin with; "Yes, but what about ... " I encourage you not to try to figure out all the answers before you affirm your total trust in God. Either He is in charge or He is not. Which do you believe? Maybe it will be necessary for you to pause and pray, repenting of the sin of unbelief. Maybe it will be necessary to acknowledge that you have believed the lie that your choices are capable of thwarting God's eternal purposes for your life.

*Dear Father,*

_____

_____

_____

_____

*Amen*

# It Really Does "All Work Together"

When we have made a decision that we believe was a mistake, it is usually hard to see through the results and recognize the hand of God in our circumstances. The enemy knows that once we feel that our actions have caused us to misstep so that we come to believe that we have somehow stepped out of God's will, a sense of intimacy with our Father becomes very difficult.

Many Christians have been put into spiritual bondage by believing the lie that they have made wrong choices that cannot be overcome. Before I understood the truth of our loving Father's sovereignty, I would sometimes say, "You can't unscramble eggs." But the truth of the matter is that God *can* unscramble eggs! He takes the choices of your lifetime and orchestrates them into the overall symphony of life that He has written for you.

I indicated at the beginning of this week's study that there are things I would do differently if I had them to do over again. It's true, *I* would. However, I can't write the story over again. Given that fact, I must choose to simply rest with confidence in the One who directs this unfolding McVey drama. I don't understand some things about my own story, but one day I will. Until then, my only viable option is to trust.

## THE DARK THREADS OF LIFE

Someone has noted that even the most beautiful tapestries have dark threads interwoven within the pattern made by the designer. God can take the dark threads of foolish choices you have made and use them in the tapestry of your life. He is not limited by anything you have ever done. Nothing caught Him by surprise. The Bible says that in God's book there were "written all the days that were ordained for [you], when as yet there was not one of them" (Psalm 139:16). Someone once asked, "Did it ever occur to you that nothing ever occurs to God?" We aren't big enough to spoil the story of our lives that God has written.

Think about your lifetime for a moment. How would you divide the years you have lived thus far? Maybe you would divide the segments of your lifetime by the jobs you have held; by the places you have lived, or by where you were in school at the time. Perhaps there is another way you would divide your lifetime. In the space below, identify the phases of life as you see them in your own life, from the time you were born until now.

> *God can take the dark threads of foolish choices you have made and use them in the tapestry of your life.*

1. _____

2. _____

3. _____

4. _____

5. _____

Maybe you didn't need all five spaces or maybe you added more. The key here is to identify the distinct sections of time in your life that you would call "a chapter in my life."

Looking over these chapters of your lifetime, identify choices you made in each time period that you afterwards regretted.

1. _____

2. _____

3. _____

4. _____

5. _____

If you couldn't think of mistakes you made during each of the periods you identified, that is okay. If you are like most of us, you were at least able to identify a few times in life when you made choices that you later came to believe were mistakes.

Look at the mistakes you have identified. How did you feel when you realized you had made a decision you wished you could rescind? What did you do to try to resolve the situation?

Looking back on each of these incidents, identify the way God brought you through the situation:

1. _____

2. _____

3. _____

4. _____

5. _____

The purpose for this exercise is to cause you to see that God has been faithful in every situation you have faced. Even if the outcome of your wrong choice wasn't the happy ending you wanted, you have seen your Father's faithfulness to guide you through it and enable you to go forward with life, trusting Him.

*Week Three*

## LIFE ISN'T JUST A MATTER OF CHANCE

The things that have happened in your life didn't just take place coincidently. They are all a part of a divine story. When Christians get to heaven and enjoy by sight the reality of the union we now share with Christ by faith, we will clearly see that our lives were nothing less than a love story depicting the intimate relationship we have with Jesus.

As with any love story, there are highs and lows while the story unfolds. There are times when one following the saga might wonder if the lovers relationship is going to last. Will he be able to keep her? Will she turn away and give her love to another? However, the author of the story knows full well how it is all going to end, because he decreed it to be so. Those who watch may be alarmed at times during the telling of the tale, but not the author.

*As with any love story, there are highs and lows while the story unfolds.*

He simply enjoys the expression of his own creative skills as it is played out before him. He knows, that in reality, the story is already finished.

The flow of events in your life aren't the result of random choices you have made. Your Father has overseen every aspect of your life and used each decision to get you to where you are today. What may look like mistakes have really been an integral part of the your story. Nothing has happened by chance.

You are familiar with the promise in God's Word found in Romans 8:28:

*And we know that God causes all things to work together for good to those who love God, to those who are called according to His purpose.*

Note that not all things seem good, but they do "work together" for good in our lives. You wouldn't want to eat the individual ingredients that go into baking a cake, but throw them all together, stick them in the oven and turn up the heat and, in time, something wonderful emerges.

That's how it is with the story of your life. While we move through this divine drama we identify as our lifetime on earth, there will be peaks and valleys. There will be times when we think we have made choices that spoil the whole story, but the Author and Finisher of our faith has already completed His work and has sat down to enjoy the fruit of His labor. (See Hebrews 12:2) As participants in the divine romance, we will enjoy this time-bound segment of the story much more if we simply believe that He indeed has finished writing the script and will see to it we are on our mark and know our lines by heart.

Tomorrow we will consider an important person in the Bible who appeared to have made a big mistake, but was actually fulfilling God's purpose. As you end your time of study today, maybe it would be good to look back over the incidents you noted that you believed were mistakes. Compare them with the way your Father brought you through them.

Nothing is going to change in your future. You will make decisions that will lead to a satisfying outcome and you will make choices that you later regret. Either way, your Father is walking with you, guiding through each step of your journey.

End your time today with a prayer, thanking Him for His faithfulness through every walk of life. Affirm the truth of Romans 8:28 as it applies to the unique circumstances of your own life.

*Dear Father,*

_____

_____

_____

_____

_____

*Amen*

# DAY FIVE

# Trust When You Don't Understand

As your study this week comes to a close, it is important that you reach the place where you resolve to trust your Father in every circumstance of life. This is a mile marker in life that you must pass if you are going to reach your intended destination of intimacy with God. It should be clear to you by now that no matter what decisions you may or may not have made, nothing you have ever done or ever will do is going to put you on a side road in life.

Your Father has been overseeing every detail of your life since the day you were born. What may have looked like mistakes that did irrevocable and permanent damage to the life-track God designed for you are, in reality, stepping stones that He uses to accomplish His purposes.

Once you realize and embrace that fact, it opens the door wide to experience intimacy with your Father at a deeper level. If we are constantly looking at our own circumstances, wondering if we are in the right place, doing the right thing, we can't focus our full attention on Him. If, however, we put to rest the notion that we are on a detour road in life, we become free to allow all our energies and focus of life to be absorbed into the loving relationship we share with God.

## MAKING SENSE OF IT ALL

God exists in what an anonymous author from the fourteenth century called "The Cloud of Unknowing." His frame of reference is so beyond ours that we simply can't consistently understand His ways in this world or even in our own lives. Even the most spiritually mature among us often find ourselves asking, "What's God up to here? What is going on in this situation? What does this circumstance mean?"

Sometimes, we can look backward in time and understand His working in our circumstances and see what He was doing at the time, even though it didn't make sense then. However, much of the time we simply can't make sense out of life's mysteries. Isaiah 55:8 says, "My thoughts are not your thoughts, Nor are your ways my ways, declares the LORD."

*Much of the time we simply can't make sense out of life's mysteries.*

We only have two options – resist God and wallow in constant frustration and confusion or else submit to His sovereign control, even though we don't always understand. Obviously, to choose the first option will block any sense of intimacy with God. The pathway toward intimacy with Him is trust.

An examination of the lives of those in Scripture who were greatly used by God shows that they all made choices that some might have called a mistake at the time. Trace the hand of God's guidance in their lives to the end and you will discover that what initially looked like a wrong choice became an integral part of the fulfillment of His plan for their lives. Remember, when you are the one in the midst of a situation, it is sometimes hard to see the whole picture. God, on the other hand, doesn't only see the whole picture – He painted it.

Consider the life of Joseph. You will need your Bible at hand now to answer a few questions about him. He is a good example of a person who could be judged to have made fatal mistakes, but whose choices God used to accomplish His purpose.

In Genesis 37:1-11, the Bible records a dream that God caused Joseph to have. It was a dream that revealed God's intentions to promote him to a place of great leadership. Read the passage of Scripture and answer the question: What was the response of his family when he told them about the dream he had?

_____

List in chronological order the results that happened in Joseph's life because he made the decision to tell his brothers about the dream God gave him: (Use the following verses to identify the answers.)

1. Genesis 37:18-28

_____

Then, when he was taken to Egypt:

2. Genesis 39:7-20

_____

While imprisoned, he interpreted the dreams of various men (see Genesis 40) and finally interpreted a dream of the Pharaoh himself. As a result of Joseph interpreting the Pharaoh's dream:

3. Genesis 41:39-41

_____

4. Genesis 45:1-8

_____

> *When Joseph told his brothers about the dream God gave him, was it a mistake?*

When Joseph told his brothers about the dream God gave him, was it a mistake? As a result of telling them, they sold him into slavery. He was carried to Egypt where he was put into prison because he wouldn't yield to the seduction of Potifer's wife. In prison, he interpreted the dreams of various men until word finally reached the Pharaoh. When Joseph interpreted one of his dreams, Pharaoh promoted him to second in command in all of Egypt. When famine struck the land of Egypt and Joseph's brothers came there, he was able to meet their needs completely.

Being able to look back at this historical event, we can see the whole picture. Joseph didn't have that benefit when he was living through it. Based on what you know of this story today:

1. Did Joseph make a mistake telling his brothers about the dream? _____

2. What was the ultimate outcome of the progression of events that followed his telling them about his dream?

_____

When Joseph was sitting in the dungeon, he would have understandable reason to question the wisdom of having told his brothers about his dream. He certainly could have thought it was a terrible mistake, but we know it wasn't. His decision to tell them was the first is a series of steps that would ultimately lead him to becoming the Prime Minister of Egypt.

Don't think for a minute that you have made foolish choices that necessitate that you now have to settle for second best in your life. The lifetime of a Christian simply doesn't work that way. God is bigger than any and every decision you will make. If you have the ability to decide and do anything that leaves Him frustrated because it was your way and not His that was accomplished, His strength and His purposes become subordinate to yours. God submitting His sovereign plan to our whimsical and volatile decisions? No way.

> *God is bigger than any and every decision you will make.*

The Bible is rich with illustrations through the lives of its characters of how God's purposes are still fulfilled despite what appears to be wrong choices. As we have seen, Joseph's decision to tell his family about his dream led to a series of apparent disasters, but in the end those very disasters became the stepping-stones that led him to fulfill his destiny.

John was exiled on Patmos for preaching the gospel. He may well have thought that he might have used more discretion about when to speak and when to keep quiet considering that nothing so abruptly ends a man's preaching ministry than to be left alone on a deserted island. However, we know in retrospect that had he not gone to Patmos we might never have received the book of the Revelation.

When Paul and Barnabas disagreed about whether or not John Mark should be given a second chance after bailing out on the first mission trip he took with them, they ended up disagreeing so strongly that they each went their separate ways. Was it a mistake? Some might have thought it was

*Week Three*

a shame that two strong preachers couldn't come to an agreement about the matter, but the Holy Spirit used it to multiply the preaching of the gospel by sending them in two separate directions.

Even Jesus was warned by Peter not to go to Jerusalem, but He went there anyway. The result of that decision was His own crucifixion. If the jury of His disciples had put His decision to a vote, every one of them would have said it was a grave mistake. You know, though, that what looked like a mistake was in fact a mission directed by Almighty God Himself.

The point of these illustrations from the New Testament is that we need to be careful not to underestimate the ability of our Sovereign God to accomplish His purpose for our lives regardless of times we may think we have totally blown it. It may look like a jumbled mess to us, but it all makes perfect sense to Him.

> *We need to be careful not to underestimate the ability of our Sovereign God.*

As we end this week of study together, my prayer is that you have come to the place where you realize that every choice you have made in life has been noted and superintended by a Sovereign God. You haven't messed up anything that God either hasn't or can't redeem. Understanding this fact is an important mile marker in moving forward in your journey toward intimacy with God. As you end this week's study, will you resolve to stop beating yourself up over decisions you believe have caused your life to jump track? Will you affirm to Him in prayer that, whether you can see it or not, you trust that He has been and is even now directing your life to ensure that everything is accomplished through you that He wants to do?

Write your prayer in the space below, renouncing your doubts about His ability to redeem any wrong choices you may have believed you made and affirm your trust that He is able to do everything in and through you that He wants to do.

Dear Father,

_____

_____

_____

_____

_____

_____

_____

_____

*Amen.*

# EXPERIENCE GOD'S HUG
# IN TIMES OF
# PERSONAL CRISIS

## DAY ONE

# *Understand That You Haven't Been Singled Out*

September 11, 2001 will forever be remembered as the darkest day in our nation's history to date. In an instant, thousands of lives were snuffed out by cowardly actions orchestrated by a mad man on the other side of the world. When our President called the nation to prayer, one lady responded to a CNN news interviewer saying, "Pray? To whom? To a God who would stand by and watch something like this happen without stopping it? I will *not* pray!"

As things progressed in the immediate days that followed the terrorist's attacks, there were more public prayers said and more said about prayer than anytime in recent American history. While this cynic's attitude wasn't representative of most of the people in our country, it did reflect a pervasive and nagging question in many people's minds, including Christians. It is the age old question which asks how a loving God could allow such horror to happen to so many innocent people.

Why does a sovereign God appear to sit idly by and watch while tragic events happen in this world? In a message at the National Cathedral in Washington, D.C. three days after the attack on our country, on a day designated as a "Day Of Prayer And Remembrance," Dr. Billy Graham said:

*How do we understand something like this? Why does God allow evil like this to take place? Perhaps that is what you are asking right now. You may even*

*Week Four*

97

*be angry at God. I want to assure you that God understands these feelings that you may have. We've seen so much on our television, heard on our radio – stories that bring tears to our eyes and make us all feel a sense of anger. But God can be trusted, even when life seems at its darkest.*

"God can be trusted, even when life seems at its darkest." Do you believe that to be true? Can we honestly believe that God loves us when life itself seems to be imploding? Perhaps there is no time in our lives that we *feel* less loved by God than when we are facing days of overwhelming difficulties. It doesn't take tragedy on a national scale for the average Christian to wonder about the legitimacy of God's compassion.

To be able to continue on your journey toward intimacy with God, you can't avoid passing this fourth mile marker. Your attitude about trusting your Father in hard times is a very important factor in how much you sense His love as you move through life.

> *God loves us when life itself seems to be imploding.*

Facing a particularly hard personal problem in his life, a friend said to me one day, "I wouldn't let *my* children go through something like this, if I had the power to prevent it. So why is God allowing me to face this problem if He loves me and has the power to stop it?" The question is a legitimate one and deserves an answer. How can we experience genuine intimacy with a God who allows us to go through personal circumstances that sometimes threaten to shake the very foundation of our faith? When a person is hurting and his faith seems to offer no relief from the pain, what is he to conclude about God's love?

During your study this week, we will examine the topic of personal problems. As you move through the week, it is important to be willing to have your mind be changed and your heart be touched by the reality of the fact that although our Heavenly Father never promised that we won't have hardships in our lives, He does promise that He is with us in the midst of whatever crisis we may face and He will sustain us, carrying us safely to the other side of the problem.

## WHY DID THIS HAVE TO HAPPEN?

A big deterrent to experiencing intimacy with God is getting bogged down in "the why" of our problems. It is a normal response when we face painful circumstances to want to understand the meaning behind them. As Christians, we do believe that all things work together for good to those who love the Lord. We simply want to know *how* our particular problem is going to be useful in our lives. We think that if we can just understand why it has happened, it will be easier to bear. When we can make no sense out of our situation, it sometimes becomes hard to experience a sense of intimacy with God at the emotional level. We know in our minds that He loves us, but in the midst of our misery it certainly doesn't feel like it!

There are many reasons why problems may come into our lives, but today I want you to zero in on one that fits us all. Generally speaking, the reason we have trouble is simply because problems are a part of life. It's that simple. If you want to consciously experience intimacy with your Father during your times of pain, you need to get the notion out of your mind that you have somehow been singled out and picked on through your troubles. As hard as it may be to accept, when trouble comes your way, the short and succinct reason for it is one thing: That's life. You can over-think the whole matter and drive yourself to the point of despair in search of an answer that satisfies you. Whether we like it or not, we live in a world of hurt.

> *The reason we have trouble is simply because problems are a part of life.*

The seed of sin planted in this world in the Garden of Eden continues to bear fruit until now. In the general sense, human suffering is a result of the fall of man. When we get home to heaven there won't be any more pain, (see Revelation 21:4) but for the time being we still live on foreign soil, where pain goes with the territory. My wife, Melanie, has always detested seafood, but when we visit Asian countries, where fish is a staple part of their national diet, she simply has to deal with it. There is no other choice. When you are in the culture, you adapt.

Pain is a part of the cultural fiber of this short earth-life and no amount of faith is going to change that fact. Standing at ground zero in his own personal disaster, Job once noted, "man is born for trouble, as sparks fly upward" (Job 5:7). He recognized that, at best, life "is short lived and full of turmoil" (Job 14:1).

The fact that one may be a Christian doesn't exempt him from problems. Consider the word of Jesus, Himself. Read John 16:33. What two things did He tell you about the troubles you will experience in this life?

Week Four

In the world you will have _____.

Take courage, though, because I have _____ _____ _____.

Faith in Christ doesn't insulate us from the stinging experiences of life. It does, however, equip us to face our problems with confidence that His loving attention will guide us through those difficult circumstances. Faith seldom answers the "why" of our problems, but instead offers the answer to "how" when we wonder about surviving our circumstances. Based on what He said in John 16:33, what do you see as the answer regarding how to face the troubles that come into your life?

_____

_____

I hope the answer you gave in the space above focuses on the importance of trusting Jesus Christ as you move through your troubles. The "how" to survive our circumstances is really a Who.

As you end your study time today, take the time to reflect on your own lifestyle and circumstances. What is the most pressing trial you face right now?

_____

_____

> *God loves you and wants you to be aware of Him walking with you through your struggles.*

You can be assured of one thing: your problems aren't because God is angry with you. He loves you and wants you to be aware of Him walking with you through your struggles. As you end your study, pause here and write a prayer to your Father expressing your trust in Him concerning the problems you face. You may not feel like expressing your faith in Him, but I encourage you to do it by faith. In time, your feelings will catch up with your profession. To grow in intimacy with God, it is important to act on what you know, not what you may feel.

*Dear Father,*

_____

_____

_____

_____

*Amen*

# Day Two

## Hold Onto The Truth

Steve, you need to get to the hospital immediately. There's been an accident." I'll never forget that day. The words caused my blood to run cold. "Andrew has fallen at work...broken back...brain hemorrhage..." My wife's words trailed off beyond my conscious thoughts as my mind struggled to comprehend what I was hearing about my son. I hung up the telephone and rushed from my office to the hospital.

"The situation is very serious," the doctor told us. "Our hospital isn't equipped to handle extensive injuries of this nature, so we are preparing to transfer him to another hospital, where they are better equipped." In the moments that followed, we learned that our twenty-year-old son had fallen from scaffolding on the construction site where he was working at the time. We were told that it might be days before the long-term effects of his injury would be known. He could be paralyzed; he might be mentally incapacitated; he may not even live. These were the possibilities outlined to us in a short conference with the doctor before getting into our car to follow the ambulance that carried him.

As we drove across town in silence, tears streamed down our cheeks. I had commented at times over the years about how suddenly life can change, but this was one scenario I had never imagined. As we pulled into the emergency room parking lot and stopped the car, I reached over and took Melanie's hand. She looked up at me through teary eyes. "We don't know what's going to happen in here today," I said. "Andrew may not live. He may be a paraplegic. He might be mentally retarded from now on. But before we go in here, can we be in agreement on one thing? No matter what happens with all of this – can we go into this hospital agreeing that God is God, and God is good?" Melanie nodded her head, indicating yes. We got out of the car and walked into the hospital, holding hands.

The days that followed were not easy ones. Andrew bled inside his swelling brain for several days. There was a nine hour operation on his broken back. There were thirty days in the hospital, then three long years of therapy. To the glory of God, He did recover and today lives a relatively normal lifestyle with little residual effects from the accident.

"Why *me?*" we may sometimes be tempted to ask, but the more logical question is, "Why *not* me?" "Accidents" happen; people are injured and sometimes even die. Being a Christian won't prevent these kinds of circumstances. To believe that because we are trusting Christ we will be shielded from suffering is a misconception of how life works. It is an erroneous belief that will cause doubt and confusion when troubles do come, as they most certainly will.

> *To believe that because we are trusting Christ we will be shielded from suffering is a misconception of how life works.*

An important part of the journey toward deeper intimacy with God is to prepare for disaster in advance. Just like you don't start out on a long trip in your car without checking your air pressure, fluid levels, and making sure you have a spare tire, neither does it make sense to move ahead through life without having taken care of a few fundamental aspects of preparation.

The necessary preparation for moving through the days of our lives in confidence is to be equipped with specific truths that ensure life's journey will be safer. The following is a checklist that will serve you well if you can carry these truths through life with you.

## 1. Life Can Turn On A Dime

When I received the call that our son's life was in the balance, it came as a complete shock to me. When the Apostle Paul went to Asia to preach the gospel, he too encountered unexpected problems. Note how he describes his circumstances in 1 Corinthians 1:8:

*Week Four*

*But I would not have you to be ignorant, brethren, of the afflictions which came to me in Asia.*

Paul wrote that troubles came to him. He was going along, minding his own business, and suddenly, here came trouble. Have you had that kind of experience in your life? Have you known situations when life seemed normal and then, out of nowhere, something terrible happened to you: What was that event?

_____

_____

You have seen, then, that life really can turn on a dime. One moment, everything is fine. The next, it seems like your world is unraveling.

How does this fact facilitate intimacy with God? The recognition of this truth nurtures an attitude in us that promotes intimacy with Him. It reminds us that we are not in charge of our own lives. God is in charge. The notion that we have everything under control in life is never anything more than an illusion. Accidents can happen, divorce can occur, people can die, careers and life savings can be lost, or disease can strike. There are a multitude of unpredictable possibilities than can take place in your life at any moment. Recognizing this reality encourages an attitude of dependency on the One who is in control of every detail of our lives.

> *We are not in charge of our own lives. God is in charge.*

## 2. Decide What You Believe Before Trouble Comes

Melanie and I reaffirmed that God is sovereign and good as we sat in the parking lot of the hospital where our son had been carried by ambulance. We weren't trying to decide whether or not God is good at that moment. We were simply affirming what we already knew to be true.

The time to settle your belief about the goodness of God is now, not when the bottom drops out on life. The pain of circumstances can easily tempt anybody to question the basic goodness of God. Overwhelmed by the horror of tragedy, it doesn't feel like He is good and circumstances don't cause it to look that way either. That is why it is necessary to settle this issue before trouble comes into your life.

Are you willing to sign your name beneath the following declaration of faith? If you are, do so:

*Father, I know that the circumstances of life can instantly change. What seems predictable to me is, in reality, only known by You. I realize that the sense that I am in control of my life is only an illusion. Anything and everything can change overnight. I acknowledge that I'm not the one in control of my life. You are. Right now, at this very moment, I affirm that You are God and You are good. Whatever my future holds, I will trust You. In times of crisis, remind me of this moment and keep me from questioning Your goodness then. I know you are good and I will cling to Your goodness all the days of my life, whatever they may bring.*

Signed: _____    Date: _____

## 3. Know That Trusting God Doesn't Mean That Circumstances Will Change

After Melanie and I affirmed our faith in God's goodness, a long and trying road lay ahead for us. Our son's surgery, rehabilitation and recovery lasted for years. On the day of his accident, his life changed and so did ours.

Faith in God doesn't mean you can write the ending to your own story. The Author and Finisher of our faith has already written your story and, from the eternal perspective, it is a beautiful one. You may not see the beauty in the story written for you until you get to heaven, but be assured that its beauty will eventually be realized.

> *Faith in God doesn't mean you can write the ending to your own story.*

The tendency we all have is to think that if we commit our troubling situations to the Lord, He will resolve them to our satisfaction. The reality is that sometimes He does and sometimes He doesn't. He always does the best thing and He is the one who defines what is best. Sometimes it all boils down to whether or not we will really trust Him. To say we trust our Father is one thing when our journey through life is smooth. To trust Him when the road is bumpy and we feel that life, as we know it, is in peril is another matter altogether. The truth of the matter is that He can be trusted, whether our circumstances change or not.

Is there an ongoing problem in your life that hasn't been resolved despite all your efforts and prayers? Have you grown weary from the wearing-down effect that your troubles have had in your life? End your study today with a prayer that affirms your trust in your Heavenly Father. You signed the declaration of trust in Him earlier in today's study, but when you are facing trying circumstances, you can't express your faith too often. Expressing your faith strengthens it and helps foster a stronger sense of dependence upon Him.

Don't believe the lie that to express faith in God when you don't feel it is hypocritical. A hypocrite is somebody who acts like they are something they aren't. You are a child of God. You do have faith in Him, whether you feel it at every moment or not. Act like who you are and affirm your faith. Keep doing it, knowing that whatever happens externally in your life, your Eternal Father is trustworthy. Don't try to understand Him. Just trust Him.

*Dear Father,*

_____

_____

_____

_____

*Amen*

# Our Pain Draws Our Focus Toward Our Father

So far this week you have learned two important aspects about experiencing intimacy with your Heavenly Father during times of personal crisis. You have seen that troubles don't come to you because you've been singled out. Tragedy doesn't come into our lives because God is angry with us. He isn't. To think otherwise will rob you of conscious intimacy with God.

Yesterday, we examined the importance of becoming settled in our minds about our belief system. In the midst of painful circumstances, we can still know intimacy with God by recognizing an important fact – our circumstances are *not* an indication of how God feels about us. If we believe that our present situation in life is indicative of God's love for us, we will become disheartened and wonder if God is absent when troubles come. Paul spoke to the issue of how our troubles relate to God's love for us in Romans 8:38-39:

*For I am convinced that neither death, nor life, nor angels, nor principalities, nor things present, nor things to come, nor powers, nor height, nor depth, nor any other created thing, will be able to separate us from the love of God, which is in Christ Jesus our Lord.*

God's final word on how He feels about you is the finished work of Jesus Christ on the cross, not whatever circumstances you may be facing at any given time. Jesus, Himself, was "a man of sorrows, and acquainted with grief" (Isaiah 53:3). If you want to understand God's attitude toward you, stare into the face of the Crucified One, who proved that He would rather die than live without you. By choice He committed Himself to the cruelty of crucifixion, driven there by a divine passion for you that set His heart ablaze with resolve to do whatever was necessary to ensure that you would be His forever. The strongest strand in the cord of truth that will sustain any Christian who suffers is the realization that Jesus Christ loves you with an eternal passion that can never be extinguished, or even diminished.

## EXPERIENCING HIM IN OUR SUFFERING

Salvation is not a matter of Jesus Christ coming into *our* lives. That perspective is a self-centered viewpoint that makes man the focal point in regeneration. To become a Christian means that we enter into *His* life. Our old lives are put to death (see Galatians 2:20; Romans 6:1-6; Colossians 3:3) and we then receive the indwelling Christ, in whom we live from that day forward. (See Acts 17:28)

*Jesus Christ loves you with an eternal passion that can never be extinguished, or even diminished.*

Few Christians resist the biblical teaching that Christ wants to express His life through them. They are attracted to the idea of living victoriously, of possessing spiritual peace, supernatural power, as well as other identifying characteristics of the Christ life. All of these are indeed characteristic of the lifestyle of those who abide in Christ, but there is another trait of His life that lacks luster to many modern Christians. It is the element of suffering.

When you entered into Christ, you came into union with every aspect of His life. Suffering isn't an insignificant part of living in Him, but is one of the most effective ways that the Holy Spirit teaches us our true identity in Christ. It is often through the experience of suffering that God carries us deeper and deeper into an understanding of who we are in Him and who He is in us. How does this happen? Perhaps an illustration from my own life will help explain.

Several years ago I had taken a shower early one morning. I slid the shower door open to step out of the shower when somehow it suddenly jumped off its track. The door instantly fell right to the floor with its edge landing straight across the top of my big toe, like a guillotine. (I probably wouldn't become a war hero in battle, if this experience were indicative of my potential.)

When the door hit my toe, I felt a mental jolt in my brain as if someone had just shot me in the head. I looked down at my toe and saw a deep gash, which was now pouring out blood. I jumped out of the shower into the bedroom on one foot and, knowing I was going to need stitches, called for Melanie to come.

I'm glad my wife already adored me because when she walked into the bedroom and saw a naked, soaking wet man with an anguished expression jumping up and down on one foot while holding the other with both hands – with blood gushing from between his fingers, it probably didn't do anything to validate my masculinity to her. With Melanie's help, we dried me off, put on my clothes and drove to the hospital emergency room where I received the stitches needed for my toe.

At the time my toe was cut, everything else in life lost its significance to me. I didn't care about conflicts in the Middle East, famine in Africa, or even the spiritual condition of our own country. Only one thing mattered to me at that moment. You might say that, right then, my whole life was a big toe. My only consuming thought was, "I need a doctor *now*." I didn't want to bleed to death and have to tell the martyrs in heaven that I got there because of a toe cut by a shower door. I've never read about anybody being laughed out of heaven and I didn't want to be the first.

*Suffering causes us to become consumed with the desire to experience Jesus Christ!*

Seriously, I find humor now in thinking back on this incident, but it wasn't funny at the time. My pain served one purpose with extreme efficiency – it caused me to want to see the doctor. That is the way in which real suffering works in the lives of Christians. Suffering causes us to become consumed with the desire to experience Jesus Christ! It makes us want to see Him, to hear His voice, to feel His touch in our circumstances. This strand in the cord of eternal truth about suffering will sustain the Christian who clings to it. Our pain points us toward Jesus Christ!

Suffering brings the indwelling life of Christ into our lives in a *manifest* way, enabling us to sense Him, by faith to *see* Him in ways that are seldom experienced in calmer days. When I cut my toe, I became oblivious to everything except my immediate need and my desire for the one who could meet that need.

That's how it is in our grace walk. God uses the severe problems of life to bring our focus to bear on Jesus. For the believer's thoughts to turn to Christ in our suffering is as natural as my thoughts turning toward the doctor when I had my accident. Suffering has a way of immediately distancing us from the incidental matters of life that distract us from Jesus Christ. When a believer hurts, deep from within, at the very core of our being, is the heartfelt cry, *"Abba!* Daddy!" (See Romans 8:15)

When *Abba's* babies hurt, He is intensively involved. Sometimes our pain is so great that it cannot be clearly explained in words. At other times, we just don't have the energy. People that aren't feeling well often want help, but at times when a person is *critically* ill, they often want to be left alone even though they may need intensive care. When we cry out to *Abba,* he hears, but there are times when we can't even cry out for His help. At those times,

> *the Spirit also helps our weakness; for we do not know how to pray as we should, but th Spirit Himself intercedes for us with groanings too deep for words: and He (Abba) who searches the heart knows what the mind of the Spirit is, because He intercedes for the saints according to the will of God. And we know that God causes all things to work together for good to those who love God, to those who are called according to His purpose (Romans 8:26-28),*

God loves you so much that He will *always* work in your circumstances when you suffer. Don't think that because He doesn't eliminate the problem, help isn't being given. Sometimes His most helpful acts in our lives occur when He goes with us *through* our circumstances instead of delivering us out of them. I have sometimes prayed about various situations, saying, "Father, this hurts too much for it to be wasted. Please accomplish the most good that possibly can be done in this situation."

> *God loves you so much that He will always work in your circumstances when you suffer.*

As you end today's study, think about a time when you have faced a serious crisis in your life. In the space below, describe how your Father brought you through the trial. Maybe your situation didn't end in the way you wanted it to be resolved. Perhaps you are even going through a painful trial even now. Be honest about your feelings and speak plainly about how God has revealed Himself to you in the midst of the problem.

_____

_____

_____

_____

_____

Read what you have written above and talk to your heavenly Father about it. Ask Him to enable you to see your problem through the lens of His love instead of judging His love by the details of your painful situation.

# DAY FOUR

## Depend On The Comfort Of Your Father's Love

*I*n order to go forward in your journey into intimacy, it is important to avoid seeing your painful circumstances in a negative way. If you see your personal crisis in your life as a bad thing, your instinct will be to fight against it in order to bring the situation to an end at any cost. If, on the other hand, you recognize that your loving and sovereign Father is in control of the details of your life, you will be positioned to receive benefits from the trial you face.

Your troubles may not feel like they could be good, but your Father will certainly accomplish good through them. The manifestation and outworking of the indwelling Christ is God's goal in our suffering. As author Watchman Nee pointed out, it is only when the alabaster box containing the precious, aromatic ointment is *broken* that its beautiful fragrance can fill the environment. (See Mark 14:3-9) God continually works to break us of any hope that *we* have life under control, so that we will experience life under *His* control. It is in this breaking process, facilitated by suffering, that self-reliance is set aside and the fragrance of Christ is released from within.

If you have ever prayed for God to use your life for His glory, it should come as no surprise when suffering comes. As in the days of John the Baptist, "He must increase and [we] must decrease." That only happens as we hand over the deed to our lives, surrendering complete ownership to Him.

God loves us so much that He will rescue us from *ourselves*. It is often a cruel irony that the enemy whispers to us during our trials, telling us that God must not care when, in reality, the direct cause for our pain is because God *does* care.

The Apostle Peter wrote:

> *"Beloved, do not be surprised at the fiery ordeal among you, which comes upon you for your testing, as though some strange thing were happening to you; but to the degree that you share the sufferings of Christ, keep on rejoicing; so that also at the revelation of His glory, you may rejoice with exaltation" (1 Peter 4:12-13).*

It is normal for the believer who hungers for God to experience suffering, for in his pain he will come to know "the revelation of His glory." What is this glory that Peter said will cause us to become so excited that we can't contain ourselves once it is revealed to us? Read 1 Corinthians 1:27 to learn the answer.

_____

_____

The Apostle Paul defined this glory when he wrote, "*Christ in you*, the hope of glory." This glory is the life of Christ inside you. The revelation of His glory happens when the Holy Spirit causes the Christian to supernaturally understand the reality of his union with Jesus. Christ is not simply *in* your life; He *is* your life!

Understanding that Christ is our life source will arm the Christian to face anything. We come to realize that we can do all things through Christ, who strengthens us. The fiery trials that come into our lives become the backdrop upon which the life of Jesus Christ can be seen in us in the same way that a brilliant diamond best reflects its beauty against a black background.

Sometimes suffering is renounced and rebuked under the guise of faith, but this approach is a contradiction of Christian orthodoxy. The Apostle Paul prayed to "know Him and the power of His resurrection *and*

> The direct cause for our pain is because God does care.

*Week Four*

*the fellowship of His suffering*" (Philippians 2:10, emphasis added). What Paul prayed *for*, many today pray against. Why did Paul pray to know the fellowship of Christ's suffering? It is because He knew that suffering is a greenhouse in which fellowship with Jesus Christ can flourish.

## HEAVENLY HUGS

We have seen earlier this week that the nature of suffering creates an environment that often proves to be extremely conducive for intimacy with God. There is something about serious trouble that sensitizes us to God's presence. Problems reduce life to its most basic elements. Our troubles often seem to take us by the hand and lead us to the foot of the cross. In that sense, suffering may become our best friend at times. Never are we more fully participating in the life of Jesus Christ than when we share in His sufferings.

> *Problems reduce life to its most basic elements.*

When you hurt, Jesus Christ grieves with you in your pain. Don't make the mistake of believing that if God really cared, He would deliver you out of your painful situation. Remember that He didn't even rescue *Jesus* from the cross as He suffered, because He knew its ultimate centrality in salvation. God loves you so much that He won't take away the pain if it serves a greater purpose in your life. Instead, He will walk the path of pain with you, and in the person of the Comforter (see John 14:16) will sustain you each step of the way.

One effective tool the enemy uses against the believer is to cause us to think that God must not care about our problems. However, it is important when we are in the midst of suffering to affirm the truth declared by the Psalmist, "This I know, that God is for me" (Psalm 56:9). Reflect on that truth for a moment – God is *for me*. Do you really believe that? Once we have embraced the truth that God is for us, the details of our circumstances become subordinate to the realization that God both cares about and controls our lives.

If you affirm your faith in the message of Psalm 56:9, fill in your name in the blanks below:

*I know that God is for _____. Despite external evidence to the contrary and regardless of how I may feel at any given moment, God loves _____ and is always at work to bring Himself glory and to accomplish His purpose in the life of _____. He is concerned about _____ For that reason, I will trust Him always.*

That foundational understanding of God's concern for us then becomes the platform upon which intimacy with Him can rest. When we honestly believe that God knows and *cares* about every detail of our lives; when we understand that He is deeply touched by our weaknesses (see Hebrews 4:15); when we are convinced that He hurts when we hurt; when we *know* these things, intimate fellowship with Him will be the natural experience in our pain. Jesus Christ longs for you to *feel* His love at the darkest times of your life.

A few years ago a friend of mine experienced a horror that would be every husband's worst nightmare. Fred awakened one morning to discover that his young wife lay dead in the bed beside him. She hadn't been sick and had no known health problems. She simply went to bed one night and never woke up.

I shed tears when I heard the news of my friend's death, and then immediately began to pray for Fred. I couldn't help but project myself into his circumstance and wonder how I would ever survive if such a horrible thing were to ever happen to me. To awaken and find that your mate has died in the bed beside you during the night is beyond comprehension for most of us.

Having lunch with Fred one day, I asked him how he was doing. I was moved by the story he told me about how Jesus comforted him during one of his darkest days. "From the beginning, part of me has wanted to be alone and yet, at the same time, I have craved people and attention," Fred said. "I have felt lonely even in a crowd. Like Job, I asked God why, but He was silent in my despair. I have felt His presence in the love of my family and friends."

He continued, "About a week after Rachel's death I had dinner in the home of close friends. They showered me with love and attention and their young children lavished their affection on me. I left for home that evening, encouraged and praising God for giving me so many close friends. But when I went to bed that night, my emotions changed. I couldn't sleep. It was a very cold December and I was shivering and praying, struggling with deep despair. All I could do is to cry out from my broken heart, 'God, I need your help!'"

Fred's eyes brimmed with tears as he continued his story. "Suddenly, at that moment, I *felt* God's presence beside me. I was lying on my side and I

> *Jesus Christ longs for you to feel His love at the darkest times of your life.*

knew He was right beside me. His arms *embraced* me and a warm ocean current flowed throughout my whole body. The sensation was brief, but I felt a closeness to Him that I can't describe. I was at peace for the first time in over a week and I was able to drift off to a restful sleep. I awoke the next morning, praising God for revealing Himself to me. From that moment, I somehow knew that I could trust Him in all of my sorrow. I realized that God hadn't chosen to save me *from* my adversity, but would ultimately lead me out of it. I realize now that God was working and answering my prayer when I could see nothing but darkness."

In the arms of Jesus, Fred found the peace He so desperately needed after his wife's death. Have you ever experienced the hug of Jesus? He wants you to feel His love in every circumstance of life. I have heard some spiritual

> *Jesus wants you to feel His love in every circumstance of life.*

leaders caution believers about the danger of an overemphasis on feelings in our walk with God. While this may be a legitimate danger at times, I am convinced that many have gone to the opposite extreme and *excluded* feelings from our relationship to Christ.

Can you think of a time when you experienced comfort from Jesus that you knew was nothing less than supernatural? Describe your own experience:

_____

_____

_____

_____

The presence of the Christ who indwells us impacts us at every level of our being. To know in our minds that somebody else loves us is one thing. To *feel* that love is another matter altogether. Healthy, loving relationships impact our thoughts *and* emotions. At times when we feel like life has run over us, we need more than a rational answer. We need a hug. Jesus always stands ready to give us the emotional comfort we want.

On the day that Billy Graham spoke to our nation after the attack on the World Trade Center and The Pentagon, he closed his remarks with these words: "My prayer today is that we will feel the loving arms of God wrapped around us and will know in our hearts that He will never forsake us as we trust in Him." As you end your study today, pray and thank God for the times you have experienced His hug in the past. Ask Him to make you aware of divine comfort as you face your problems now and in the future.

*Week Four*

# DAY FIVE

## Show Yourself Some Grace

When my four children were small, occasionally the electricity would go off in our home at night. If they were still awake, I would hear a unified chorus cry out, "Daddy!" Melanie and I would walk through the dark rooms and collect them one by one and bring them back to our bed, where we would lie down with them. With all six of us in one bed, we would put our arms around the children and assure them that we were with them. Without fail, in a short time they would all fall asleep, secure in the fact that we were there, holding them in the dark.

This week you have learned that your Heavenly Father is always there for you when the lights go out in life. He has you in His arms. He is with you when you are in the dark. When you are afraid, you can feel His love and know that He cares for you. (See 1 Peter 5:7) You may be assured that, although it might be pitch black around you, the sun will shine again. Until then, just rest in *Abba's* arms, knowing that He will never let you go.

When you're standing in the middle of troubling and confusing circumstances, choose to continuously think about the reality of the love of Christ for you. Through the eyes of faith, envision Jesus wrapping His arms around you. He hugs you and softly whispers to you, "It's okay. I'm here. I love you and promise you that everything is going to be okay. Just stay here in my arms. I'll take care of you." Nothing in life provides a greater sense of peace in the face of personal sorrow than knowing that we are being held in a never-ending heavenly hug. In His arms, we find a "peace that passes understanding."

Do you believe that your Father is for you and that He will deliver you through your trials safely to the other side of the circumstance? When you embrace the truth that He does deeply love you, in spite of any painful things that may come into your life, you will find yourself moving further along the road toward deeper intimacy. If you doubt your Father's love because of painful events you have experienced, renew your mind with verses from the Bible that assure you of His great love. For instance, the Apostle Paul wrote:

> *For I am persuaded that neither life, nor death, nor ...... shall be able to separate us from the love of God in Jesus Christ our Lord. Romans 8:38-40*

*Do you believe that your Father is for you?*

Look at that passage again and circle the things listed that have threatened your awareness of the love of God. Knowing His love is the only thing that will sustain you through the crisis of life.

In a hymn he wrote in 1876, George Robinson said:

> *Things that once were wild alarms cannot now disturb my rest;*
> *Closed in everlasting arms, pillowed on the loving breast.*
> *O to lie forever here, doubt and care and self resign,*
> *While He whispers in my ear, I am His, and He is mine.*
> *While He whispers in my ear, I am His and He is mine.*

It may be an ambitious attempt, but in the space below try to write a short verse that expresses your own belief in the loving care of your Heavenly Father. If the words don't rhyme, that's okay. Do the best you can. By putting the expression of your faith in words on paper, you will find your confidence in the love of your Father to be strengthened.

_____

_____

_____

_____

## DON'T BE TOO HARD ON YOURSELF

Don't beat yourself up if you aren't moving through your personal crisis in the best possible way. Many great Christians have gone through trials without keeping their head held high and their feelings staying strong all the way.

Look at what Paul said in 2 Corinthians 2:8-9 about how he went through the trials he faced when he was in Macedonia:

> *"We don't want you in the dark, friends, about how hard it was when all this came down on us in Asia province. It was so bad we didn't think we were going to make it. We felt like we'd been sent to death row, that it was all over for us." (The Message)*

> *Many great Christians have gone through trials without keeping their head held high and their feelings staying strong all the way.*

Does it sound like he was sailing through his troubles with a conscious sense of victory? Pretend you are writing Paul a note while he was going through that situation. What would you say to him?

_____

_____

What about Job? Have you read that book of the Bible? It seems like Job spent most of the book mourning and complaining about his troubles ~ not that he didn't have a right to feel that way. If you had written Job a short note to encourage him, what would you have said?

_____

_____

Look at what you would have said to both of these men. Was your advice to them to give up faith? To shame them for thinking and feeling like they did? I suspect that your answer to them was to show them grace, to encourage them by reminding them that it would all be okay in the end. You wouldn't put them down for having normal human emotions in the circumstances they had to face.

Now, here is a *big* step that you can take to help yourself. Treat yourself the same way. That's right ~ show yourself the same grace you would show to somebody else. It's amazing how gracious we can be with other people when they go through hard times and express negative thoughts or feelings. Then we turn right around and don't cut ourselves one ounce of slack when we are in similar situations. Don't do that to yourself.

Your Father is a gracious God to all His children. It's okay if you don't handle your situation perfectly at every instant. Job really did spend considerable time talking about how life stinks, how he wished he had never been born, etc. On and on he went, but do you know what the Bible says about him? Here's the Bible's verdict:

*In all this did not Job sin with his lips (Job 2:10).*

The grace of God really is amazing. He knows we are human and is gentle and understanding with us. Psalm 103:14 says, "He knows our frame; He is mindful that we are but dust." Don't expect yourself to be *Superhuman.* Yes, you are a Christian, but you are one who lives with all the normal feelings and tendencies of a normal human being. So don't beat yourself up over that!

It's okay that you don't react at every second in the way you want to respond. When you fail, just shake it off and keep going in faith. God isn't keeping score to see how your behavior is as you move through your crisis. He is interested in your heart. When you blow it, He still knows your heart and isn't rattled because you didn't act perfectly.

Life is a process of constant growth. There are no experts when it comes to moving through the hard times of life. We cling to Christ, show ourselves grace and wait it out as we trust Him to lead us in how we act. Even the Apostle Paul didn't claim to have it down pat. He wrote in Philippians 3:13, "Friends, don't get me wrong: By no means do I count myself an expert in all this, but I've got my eye on the goal, where God is beckoning us onward ~ to Jesus."

> *It's okay that you don't react at every second in the way you want to respond.*

*Week Four*

That's it. Just keep your eyes on Jesus. Once you've done that, you've done the most anybody can do in times of personal crisis.

As you come to the end of this week's study, maybe it would be a good idea for you do two things. The first is to admit that it's okay if you don't handle troubles in a perfect way at every minute. The second is to pray and thank your Father that He doesn't require perfection from you. Faith doesn't mean that you never say a negative word or have a negative feeling. Faith means you trust Him, believing that He is going to do all He says He will do. To the extent you appropriate this reality, you will increase your speed down the road toward intimacy with Him.

# Week Five

## LOOK AT OTHERS TO SEE HOW MUCH GOD LOVES YOU

# Our Fathers Are Object Lessons Of God's Love

*I*n the past month, we have moved forward together in the journey into intimacy with God. You've passed four important mile-markers that indicate that you are making good progress toward experiencing your Father's love in a deeper way.

We are now at the halfway point in our journey together through this book. Are you applying the things you are learning to your own life? Don't simply accept the content you are reading at an intellectual level. I encourage you to pray your way along this journey so that the truths you are learning will impact you not only in your mind, but in your emotions too. God wants you to know His love at every level of your being.

This week our study will focus on learning how God loves you by seeing how He compares His love to the human relationships you have in life. We are all born with a need to be loved.

From the moment a child is born, he begins to cry. Doctors say that the physical act of crying clears mucus from his airway and causes his lungs to expand. That may be the physiological reason why he cries, but what is the psychological reason for a baby's cry? What *motivates* him to cry out as if, from the moment he is born, there is an intense need that he insists be met?

Maybe the answer to why a baby cries can best be determined by identifying what causes him to *stop* crying. The single most effective remedy for a baby's cry is to be cradled in the arms of his mother. Nurtured at the bosom of his mother, hysterical babies drift off into a peaceful sleep. Based on that fact, we might conclude that the need babies come into the world screaming to have met is the need for loving intimacy. The gentle expression of intimacy from a loving parent quells the emotional storm, and soothes him in a way nothing else can do. Watch a crying newborn as his mother takes him into her arms, speaks softly to him and cuddles him. The result is universal.

> *The need babies come into the world screaming to have met is the need for loving intimacy.*

## OUR HUNGER FOR LOVE

There is a sense in which that immediate cry to experience affectionate love will continue throughout life. By the time he reaches adolescence, the child begins to look to friends to validate his value as a person and to cause him to feel loved. During the teen years, the hunger for love explodes like fireworks, often reaching out in every direction in an attempt to be filled. The hunger to be accepted may take on the form of an extreme fashion statement or a shared affinity with his peers for the "wild music" of his day. It may be something as simple as using the lingo of his generation which is popular at the time, always an amusing and puzzling practice to the older generation, despite the fact that their parents thought the same things about them.

What is something you did during your youth to fit in with the crowd?

_____

Over the years, what was "the cat's meow" became "cool," then "groovy," then "bad," and today, "the dope," none of which offer a better substitute for the old fashioned word, "good." But that's not the point. The bottom line is that people have a default setting that causes them to do or say whatever it takes to insure that they find a place where their basic needs for love, acceptance, and value can be met.

Don't think for a moment that this cry for love ends when a person "grows up." No sane man today would be caught wearing a leisure suit, but it wasn't so many decades ago that you weren't fashionably approved if you wore otherwise. One modern dad told his young son, "In my day, we wore our baseball cap with the bill of the cap on the front of our head." "You wore it *backwards?*" the puzzled little boy replied. The truth is, that in every generation, people will do whatever it takes.

What do people in your age bracket now do to fit in with others?

_____

The hunger to feel loved never stops. From the time a child who is born today begs for his first popular toy until he is an old man driving a big, luxury car and trying to catch "the early bird special" at the old folk's cafeteria, he wants to find a place where he fits in – where he is loved, valued and accepted. The needs are normal. In fact, they are universal.

## RELATIONSHIP IS EVERYTHING

Ideally, life begins with a person being born into a home where he will be nurtured by loving parents and ends with one lifelong mate gently holding the hand of the other when the last breath is drawn. Between these starting and ending mile markers of the earth-life, we have many relationships. Each of them can help us understand something about the relationship we have with God. Every good aspect of any relationship you will ever have in this world is a way that God shows you something important. Whatever good you have ever found in *any* relationship has been the creative, artistic hand of God drawing a living picture of His love for you. That's why the Enemy tries to destroy our relationships. He understands, better than we do, that human relationships are a display case intended to show us something about the relationship that God wants to have with us. No single human relationship can make it perfectly clear. It is the combination of the good in *all* of them that give a glimpse of the believer's relationship to God through Christ Jesus.

This week we will examine some of the most important human relationships anybody will know in this life. As you consider each of these, you'll see how they demonstrate something about God's love for you.

> *Every good aspect of any relationship you will ever have in this world is a way that God shows you something important.*

## GOD AS OUR FATHER

Jesus referred to God as "Father" one hundred and eighty two times in the gospels. That is, by far, the most common way God is described by Jesus. The word brings to mind the idea of loving protection and provision. Since the beginning of mankind, fatherhood has been associated as a position of loving strength and supply.

The word "father" brings the idea of loving strength to mind. In the presence of their loving father, children feel safe. When a small child is threatened or feels afraid, the natural instinct of his heart is to cry out "Daddy!"

The thought of God being our heavenly Father is a source of comfort to many people. If you grew up in a home where your father loved you unconditionally, expressed affection and bragged on you, and gave gentle guidance and encouragement for you to be your best in every situation, then you already have a great framework for developing a clear understanding of God's love. A child's first impression of God generally develops around how he sees his own earthly father. He will often carry that underlying concept of God with him throughout life.

> *A child's first impression of God generally develops around how he sees his own earthly father.*

The reality is, though, that not everybody grew up in a home where there was a loving father. One man said to me, "In your teaching today, you talked about understanding our heavenly Father's love and acceptance for us, but that's hard for me. My father was never anything other than harsh and judgmental toward me." He made a good point. Some people grew up with a father who with an overbearing, authoritarian attitude, one who demanded nothing less than perfection of his children. Rewards were few, but punishment for failing to meet his standards came quickly. Others grew up in a house with an absentee dad, whose lack of involvement communicated a lack of concern.

God may be like your father, but it is important to also understand that God may be *nothing* like your earthly father. If you grew up in an environment that now causes the word "father" to provoke a negative response in your mind or emotions, it will be necessary to educate yourself on the Fatherhood of God. What kind of Father is God?

Phillip once said to Jesus, "Show us the Father and it will be enough for us." His request implied that he wanted to know what kind of Person God is. "Let us see Him, " he said. "Then we will know and be satisfied." Jesus responded by saying to Phillip, "he who has seen me, has seen the Father" (John 14:9) If you want to know what kind of Father God is, look at Jesus.

What would you conclude about what kind of Father God is by looking at how Jesus behaved in these verses? Write your answers in the blank space between each verse.

✎ John 13:1

✎ Matthew 8:25-26

✎ John 11:33-35

✎ Matthew 28:17-20

Do you get an idea of what kind of Father God is from these verses? Jesus said, "I and the Father are one" (John 10:30). Some people imagine God to be the hard, critical Person in the Trinity and that Jesus is the "go-between" who calms God down on our behalf. That's not true. The attitude of God is exactly the same as that of Jesus. He adores you and has committed Himself to you for all eternity.

> *If you want to know what kind of Father God is, look at Jesus.*

If you struggle with seeing God as a loving Father, it might help you to read the gospels *slowly*, pausing and writing down every positive quality you see there about the kind of Father He really is. Start with the gospel of John – the one whose writer called himself "the disciple that Jesus loved."

Nothing robs believers of joy like a distorted concept of God. As long as somebody believes that God is critiquing his every move, he will never feel free to relax and enjoy life. When we come to understand, however, that God laughs with delight every time He looks at us, (see Zephaniah 3:17) we become like the little child, who cries out, "Daddy, watch this! Watch this!" Your Daddy (*Abba*) is watching you and He is thrilled with what He sees!

As you end your study today, spend a few moments in prayer thanking your heavenly Father for His love. Ask Him to help you to better understand Him. Tell Him the things that you appreciate most about how He relates to you.

*Week Five*

# DAY TWO

## Our God Also Loves Us Like A Mother

*I*t wasn't easy for me to move beyond only relating to my heavenly Father and begin to understand God as a Mother too. I had a big hurdle to overcome. The very idea of God acting as a Mother brought back memories of my college days when I heard about people who embraced a feminist theology ~ one that thinks it's unfair to see God like a man. They went so far they actually prayed to "our Mother God." Many of these feminist theologians want to take all the masculine words about God out of the Bible. They sometimes even refer to God as "she." I've always thought that is going too far.

I grew up in a traditional, conservative home and church. It caused me to cringe to think about God in a motherly sort of way. The way I saw it was that their insistence on referring to God using feminine pronouns wasn't because they wanted to communicate another way to understand intimacy with Him, but instead because they were promoting an approach to theology that served their own political agenda. If my understanding of their motivation was right, I still wouldn't agree with what they did because of why they did it.

However, I have come to see that God really does relate to His children in maternal ways just as He does paternally. You don't need to be uncomfortable about this. Don't let this idea push a hot button in your mind. I assure you that I'm not suggesting that God is female. For that matter, God isn't male either. God is a Spirit, but in the Bible He does sometimes present Himself relating to His children in a motherly role.

Consider what God said in Isaiah 66:12-13:

*And you shall be nursed, you shall be carried on the hip, and fondled on the knees. As one whom his mother comforts, so will I comfort you.*

Circle the three verbs in this verse that tell how God relates to you like a mother. Describe what the three words mean to you in your own relationship to God.

_____

_____

God promises that when His children need comfort, He will pick us up and hold us on His hip like a mother tends to her restless baby. He will put us on His knees, play with us, gently love us, and talk to us until we are comforted.

In another verse God says:

*Can a woman forget her nursing child, and have no compassion on the son of her womb? Even these may forget, but I will not forget you (Isaiah 49:14-15).*

"Will a new mother abandon her nursing child?" God asks. "It's unlikely, but even if she would, I would never do that to you." It's not uncommon for fathers to walk out on the babies. Mothers seldom do and God *never* will.

In what ways can you compare how your own mother has loved you with the way God loves you?

_____

_____

The main characteristic of a mother that God identifies Himself with is that of being a comforter. The gentle expression of God's love soothes the hurting Christian. The Psalmist understood the motherly aspect of God

*God sometimes presents Himself relating to His children in a motherly role.*

when he said; "Surely I have composed and quieted my soul like a weaned child rests against his mother" (Psalm 131:2).

## A COMFORTING TOUCH

When I was a small child, there was a particular thing my mother did which would have an immediate effect on me. Maybe it would be after I had been hurt and was crying. Maybe it would be at times when she was simply expressing affection to me. There were probably many different situations in which it might happen, but the experience was almost transcendent for the little boy I remember. It caused me to feel at rest in a way that few things in life have ever done.

> *The gentle expression of God's love soothes the hurting Christian.*

My mother would gently stroke my hair. It was that simple. I don't remember what she said at those times. I can't even clearly describe the surrounding circumstances at any of the times she did it. I just remember her doing it – stroking my hair gently. What does stand out in my mind is how I felt in those moments. I felt love from my mother. I felt safe, accepted, *comforted*. Regardless of the circumstances, I felt like everything was going to be okay.

Maybe that habit is an inherent trait that comes with motherhood. I've seen my wife, Melanie, do the same with our children and even noticed our daughter, Amy, doing it to my grandchildren. It is a simple maternal expression of love that speaks volumes to a child.

In what ways did your own mother comfort you when you were a child?

_____

_____

What similarities do you see between your mother's comfort and the comfort God has given you during times of crisis in your life?

_____

_____

Dads don't normally comfort their children in that same way and even when they do, it doesn't have the same effect as the loving comfort of a mother. When my children were very small and would get hurt, they have ran *past* me crying many times in an urgent rush for their mother. I understood. I was a kid once too. Sometimes, only a mother will do.

You may find that your concept of God is strengthened in a way that brings a deeper sense of intimacy into your relationship with Him if you begin to think of the maternal aspects of His affections toward you. Maybe you're completely comfortable with approaching Him the way you would a Mother. Maybe, however, you find the idea of God acting as a Mother to be uncomfortable due to the traditions of your upbringing. The point here is for you to better understand intimacy with God through the considering characteristics depicted by motherhood.

Spiritual growth often requires that we choose to rise above the traditions that have influenced our lives. At times in our journey of grace, it is necessary to embrace what the Bible teaches and what the Holy Spirit shows us even though it may be uncomfortable at first. I'm not trying to cause you to change your mind about God as He relates to gender. Again I stress, God is a Spirit, not male or female. But it will help you move further down the road toward intimacy if you understand how God relates to you in motherly ways.

> *Spiritual growth often requires that we choose to rise above the traditions that have influenced our lives.*

Based on this discussion of God's love being like that of a mother, what would you say to somebody who argues that it is wrong to think of God as feminine in any sense?

_____

_____

The reason I'm pressing this point is because many people's first impulse would be to reject anything that remotely points to any feminine characteristics of God. The only thing I'm trying to do is encourage you to allow the Holy Spirit to broaden your understanding of God's role in your life so that you will know the benefit of motherly love in your relationship to Him. Intimacy between a mother and child is a unique kind of experience, different from any other love relationship we will ever know. If you want to fully understand God's love for you, it is important to know His fatherly *and* motherly qualities. It takes both to fully reveal who He is to us.

What are some other qualities of mothers not mentioned in your study today that show the kind of relationship God wants to have with you?

_____

_____

End your study time today by thinking about your own mother and how she has shown the love of God to you during your lifetime. As you pray, thank God for the way Divine Love has been revealed to you through your mother. Pray that in the future you will be made aware of times when God is showing love to you in the same way that your mother has done. As this happens, you will find that the sense of intimacy between you and God seems to be growing.

Fill in the blanks in the prayer below to express your thoughts about God loving you like a mother.

*Dear God,*

*I know you are neither male nor female, but most of your children have only seen you in terms of your Fatherhood. As I think about it, I realize that you really are like a mother in many ways.*

*I think of my own mother and the way she always would _____ and I'm reminded that you have done the same thing in my life.*

*I think about how my mother has told me _____ and I realize that you want to communicate the same thing to me.*

*I think of my mother's affection, her gentleness and her love for me and I see now that her love for me has been a small picture of your great love for me.*

*Teach me to rest in your love and to learn more about the comfort and the tenderness and compassion that you have for me.*

*I love you too and am thankful for your gentle love,*

*Amen*

# Our God Loves Us Like A Friend

Start your study today by thinking of the person in this world who has been the closest friend you have ever had in life? Describe the main characteristics of that person that caused him or her to become your best friend:

_____

_____

The French poet, Jacques Delille wrote, "Fate chooses your relations; you choose your friends." None of us decided which family we would be born into, but we do decide who we want to be our friends. Nobody wants to become friends with every person he meets. However, there are certain people that come across our paths whom we decide we would like to know better. We make the effort to establish a relationship with them and, over a period of time, deep friendships develop.

It's an amazing truth to consider that God has made a decision to become your Friend. Look back at the characteristics you used to describe the person who has been your best friend in this world. Can you see how God has those characteristics too? The fact is, though, that God is a better friend to you than any human being could ever be. As you know, human friendships don't always last a lifetime even though they may be very real for a time. God's choice to be your friend is different. He has decided that nothing will ever change the friendship He has with you. He will be your friend and love you forever.

Can you imagine that the God of the universe wants to be your friend for all eternity? To have Him as a friend is greater than any relationship you will ever have with a friend in this world. God doesn't look at you as one of the crowd among those He loves. He knows and cares about you personally.

## A PRESIDENT AND A SCHOOLGIRL

Debbie shared an experience with me not long ago that I found to be amazing. She was a junior in high school during the time that Richard Nixon was President of the United States. In one of her classes, she had an assignment to write a report on the President's wife, Pat Nixon. As she studied Mrs. Nixon's life, Debbie gained a deep respect and appreciation for her.

> *Nothing will ever change the friendship God has with you.*

One of the coincidental details of Mrs. Nixon's life that Debbie learned was that they both had the same birthday. She decided to write the First Lady and express her respect and appreciation for her. In her letter, she made her aware that they both shared the same birthday.

A short time later Debbie received a letter from Mrs. Nixon. Not a form letter, but a personal, hand written letter. Debbie decided to respond to Mrs. Nixon's letter by writing her a second time. She did and again Mrs. Nixon responded with a personal letter. What followed was that the seventeen-year-old high school girl and the President's wife became pen pals. Debbie and Mrs. Nixon wrote each other for several years.

In March of 1974, the Nixon's were invited to the opening of The Grand Old Opry in Nashville, Tennessee. The opening day also happened to coincide with Mrs. Nixon and Debbie's birthday. To her delight and surprise, the now nineteen-year-old Debbie received a letter from Mrs. Nixon, inviting her to be her guest at The Grand Old Opry. Debbie went to Nashville, where she stood waiting with visiting dignitaries to meet President and Mrs. Nixon. One snobbish woman, looked this young nineteen year old girl up and down and arrogantly asked, "And why are *you* here?" Debbie simply answered, "I'm an invited guest of Mrs. Nixon."

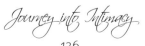

As Debbie told the story to me, she said, "I couldn't believe it. There I was as the *guest* of the guest of honor." Among all those who clamored to have a brief moment with Mrs. Nixon, nineteen-year-old Debbie Streeter was her guest and her friend.

Can you imagine such a thing? As unusual as that kind of situation might be, it's nothing compared to the friendship you have with God. It is an amazing part of the gospel of grace that God has chosen you to be His friend.

You aren't God's friend in the same sense that Mrs. Nixon and Debbie were friends. Theirs was a casual connection, but God's connection to you is very personal and deeply intimate. His desire is that the friendship you two share be the closest relationship you will ever have to anybody.

> *It is an amazing part of the gospel of grace that God has chosen you to be His friend.*

## FRIENDS KNOW EACH OTHER INTIMATELY

One benefit of an intimate friend is that there is nothing that can't be shared between them. True friendships don't disconnect because of faults each may have. Ralph Waldo Emerson said, "It is one of the blessings of old friends that you can afford to be stupid with them."

God is that kind of friend to you. Do you feel free to share the deepest and darkest aspects of your life with Him? You can, because He totally accepts you. Even if we do something stupid, His attitude toward us never changes. Understanding and believing in God's complete acceptance is a vital key in developing intimacy with him.

## FRIENDS LOVE NO MATTER WHAT

Five couples in our Grace Walk Group sat together one evening in my home. We had been singing choruses, laughing and talking, and sharing the snacks each had brought. As the time approached when we were going to pray together, one of the ladies in the group began to speak. Tears filled her eyes and her voice quivered as she said, "John (not his real name) and I need your prayers. We agreed before we arrived tonight that we would ask you to pray for us concerning a problem we have." She then began to explain how she had committed adultery and had recently confessed her sin to her husband. Tears streamed down the cheeks of both of them. Those of us in the room began to cry too as Mary (not her real name) described what had happened and the impact it had on their relationship.

After she had finished talking, my wife, Melanie, spoke first. "Mary," she said, "the first thing you need to know is that there is nothing you could ever tell us that would cause us to love you any less." As Melanie spoke, I am sure that everybody in the room felt what I felt – the presence of God with us. As she ministered loving acceptance to our friend, we were all aware of Jesus speaking through her at that moment. His gracious acceptance and gentle Spirit permeated the room.

We had John and Mary move their chairs to the center of the room, where we all gathered around them and, one by one, prayed for them. We then hugged them, held them and assured them of our love. The healing had begun.

Has there ever been a time when a friend shared something very personal with you? Describe that moment and how you responded to your friend?

_____

_____

It speaks well of your friendship that the person was willing to be completely honest with you? Intimacy requires openness. Friends don't have to impress each other. That's true with your relationship to God too. You don't have to put your best foot forward with Him. He *knows* you, *everything* about you, and still loves you completely. There is nothing you could ever tell Him that would cause Him to love or accept you any less.

> *He knows you, everything about you, and still loves you completely.*

Read this verse and underline the two things that will never happen as far as the Lord's love and compassion for you are concerned:

*"The Lord's lovingkindnesses indeed never cease, For His compassions never fail. They are new every morning. Great is [His] faithfulness"* (Lamentations 2:22-23)!

You'll never have another friend like God. How He feels about you will never change. Not ever. Nothing you do or don't do will ever change that fact.

Understanding God's total acceptance not only frees us from the prison of self-condemnation, but also empowers us to love others who have sinned. We are able to give them the same compassionate tenderness of Jesus that we ourselves have received. Those who know they have received compassion can give it. For the one who has experienced the gentle acceptance of our Friend, it is natural thing to tenderly share it with others.

God has seen the ups and downs of your life. He has seen you at your best and your worst, and yet still loves you unconditionally. He wants you to share yourself completely with Him, with complete confidence that He will not respond in criticism.

> *You'll never have another friend like God. How He feels about you will never change.*

The scorecard on your life was torn up at the cross and God has stopped keeping score on you. Your friendship with Him isn't about how you behave. Ironically, the realization of that fact is the only thing that will cause your behavior to change. Friendship with God is about enjoying each other's company. It is a relationship that will never end for all eternity. He wants you to tell Him everything and as you grow in intimacy, He will tell you more and more too.

Look at the words of Jesus:

*"I have called you friends, for all things that I have heard from my Father I have made known to you" (John 15:15).*

What does Jesus say He will do because His considers you His friend?

_____

As you walk with Him, He will reveal more and more to you about the Father until the day you see Him face to face. He is the "friend who sticks closer than a brother" (Proverbs 18:24). Emily Dickinson once said, "My friends are my estate." That is true of your relationship to Christ. He is your inheritance, a gift to you from the Best Friend You will ever have.

*Week Five*

List the top three characteristics you value in a true friend.

1._____

2._____

3._____

End this study time today by praying and thanking God for the ways He has demonstrated each of these characteristics to you in the relationship He has to you.

# DAY FOUR

# God Is The Divine Lover
# Of Your Life

So far this week, we have seen that our God loves us like a father, a mother, and a dear friend. Today we will consider what the Bible says about how His love can be compared to the most intimate relationship we will have in this world – that of a marriage partner.

Perhaps the most intimate relationship the Bible uses to identify our relationship to Christ is that of a bride and groom. The Scripture repeatedly points toward that union as a picture of the way God relates to us. In fact, the Bible says that one day we will hear a resounding invitation echoing through the universe, "The Bridegroom is coming! Come out to meet Him!" (Matthew 25:6) In that moment, we will see the One whose passion for us was so great that he thought it better to die than live without us.

The fact that God uses marriage as a picture of the kind of relationship He shares with us is usually not uncomfortable for most ladies. Men often have a difference response. Since I wrote my book, *A Divine Invitation*, where I discussed this topic at length, I've been surprised to discover the great number of men who struggle with this.

## A WORD FOR MEN

Let me direct these few paragraphs specifically to the men who read this: If you want to experience a deeper sense of intimacy with God, you might find

*Week Five*

141

it to be important that you allow the Holy Spirit to change your viewpoint about God's affectionate and tender expressions of intimacy. Sometimes men feel like their masculinity is in some way being attacked when they hear about Christ identifying Himself as the bridegroom and us as the bride.

It is important to understand that this comparison He makes isn't about gender or sexuality. It's about the way He wants us to receive His gentle expressions of love in the same way we want our wives to receive our love. If this whole idea causes you to feel uncomfortable, it would be a good idea to begin to regularly pray about it and ask God to change your thoughts and attitudes about the matter.

Learn to be comfortable with the tender love God wants you to experience. I've met men that are very uncomfortable with being hugged, even by

> *Learn to be comfortable with the tender love God wants you to experience.*

their own brother or their sons. They didn't grow up being hugged by their Dads and now they feel threatened by that kind of affection. That's not a good thing. It not only can interfere with relationships you have in this world, it can interfere with your sense of intimacy with God too. If you think affectionate expressions of love aren't important, you are fooling yourself. They *are* important – both in human relationships and in our relationship to God.

It's okay if you aren't there yet in terms of your comfort level, but I can't encourage you enough to pray to grow in this area. Then be responsive as the Holy Spirit gives you opportunities to both give and receive affection. You will find it to have a healing effect in your relationships both with other males and with God.

## Gushing Grace

Do you remember when you fell in love for the first time? You couldn't stop thinking about the one you loved. You gushed expressions of love every time you were with that person. That's how God is with you. Read Ephesians 1:7-8 in your Bible and fill in the blank in the following statement. "I have experienced the riches of God's grace which He _____ on me!"

The New Testament is saturated with descriptions of the greatness of God's love for us. In fact, even the Old Testament makes His love clear to us. The Song of Solomon is a book about the relationship between two lovers – a King and a young maiden. Its words are sometimes so intense that throughout church history there have been those who argued it shouldn't even be in the Bible. The Divine Lover made sure it was there though. It is a love poem written for you to show you how much He loves you. Here's how He expressed His love there:

*How beautiful you are, my darling. How beautiful you are! There is no blemish in you!*
*Arise, my darling, my beautiful one, and come along.*
*You have made my heart beat faster with a single glance of your eyes.*
*How beautiful you are, my love, with all your charms.*

In the space below, write your response back to God. Deliberately gush with your expression of love for Him, the way He does toward you. It's okay if your emotions aren't involved in it. Write it because you know it is true. It is a good exercise to verbally express your love to God. Expressing love with words is helpful in every relationship you have.

_____

_____

_____

You had better get used to God expressing His love to you because it's true. He says He loves you and He means it. What He says is an objective fact, whether you believe it or not. If you don't believe it now, rest assured that you will, because he is going to keep telling you how beautiful and precious you are to Him throughout eternity. One day, either now or later, the reality of His words will transform you.

## ONE PLUS ONE EQUALS ONE

Why did God choose to use the marriage relationship to show us the way He wants us to experience Him in our lives? The answer to that question can be found in the two verses below. Read them both and see if you notice the common element between them. One verse is about marriage between a man and woman and the other is about salvation, but they both point to the same thing.

> *God says He loves you and He means it.*

*"For this reason a man shall leave his father and his mother, and be joined to his wife; and they shall become one flesh" (Genesis 2:24).*

*"But the one who joins himself to the Lord is one spirit with Him"* *(1 Corinthians 6:17).*

What is the common denominator between these two verses?

_____

_____

When you became a Christian, much more happened than just having your sins forgiven.

You have been joined together in a union with God through Christ. The common denominator in the two verses above is the *union* shared between married couples and between Christians and our God.

God loves you so much that He hasn't just come into your life. It's better than that. He has brought you into *His* life. He has made you His companion for all eternity. The church is the bride of Christ. He has gone to prepare a honeymoon home for us (see John 14:1-3) and will one day take us there to spend eternity in our heavenly home!

One passage from the Bible often read at wedding ceremonies is 1 Corinthians 13. It is known as "the love chapter." As you end this study today, I want to ask you to read that chapter. Before you do, consider these words, from 1 John 4:8: *God is love.*

Since 1 Corinthians 13 is a chapter about love and the Bible tells us that God *is* love, you can know that the chapter in 1 Corinthians is really about Divine Love ~ the love that your God has for you. Read the chapter from your Bible and each time that you see the word "love," substitute the word "God" in its place. This exercise will help you to see that God is not at all like many Christians have imagined Him to be.

After you have read 1 Corinthians 13, go through your day thinking from time to time about the different ways God's love is described in that chapter. As you think about it during the day, thank Him for loving you in the specific ways described there.

# Singing And Dancing All The Way Home

As we come to the end of this week's studies, I hope you better see just how much God wants you to understand His love for you. The human relationships we have considered this week don't begin to do justice in communicating how deeply God loves you and wants you to enjoy intimacy with Him.

So many of us have a distorted concept of how God feels about us. We mistakenly believe that because our behavior isn't always what we think it needs to be that somehow that affects His attitude toward us.

Of course you know that He loves you. After all, He's God so the fact that He loves you is a given. But have you ever stopped to think about how He *feels* toward you? You know that, in human relationships, it is altogether possible to sincerely love somebody and yet still have negative feelings about them based on how they act.

Pause here for a moment and describe the way you think God has felt toward you most of your life:

_____

_____

What words did you use? There was a time when I would have used words like "frustrated, disappointed, hopeful (that I would do better)," and even "impatient." That's' what I honestly thought, but the truth is that God isn't like that. His feelings toward us don't have anything to do with our behavior. Your past or present actions don't have one iota of influence on how He feels about you.

Your God is a Loving Father, a Comforting Mother, a Faithful Friend and a Passionate Lover. However, He doesn't relate to us in those roles in the imperfect way we have experienced them in this life. He is the perfect personification of the best of each of those relationships.

Which of the following words describe what you think God is doing right now:

| | | | |
|---|---|---|---|
| _____ | Worrying | _____ | Resting |
| _____ | Laughing | _____ | Hoping things turn out well |
| _____ | Feeling anger | _____ | Singing |
| _____ | Frowning | _____ | Biting His fingernails |
| _____ | Celebrating | _____ | Loving |

You know the correct answers here. God isn't sitting up in heaven, hoping that things turn out okay down here on planet earth. If He were, He'd be worse off than we are. At least we can pray. He wouldn't even have anybody to pray to for help!

I'm joking to make a point. God is *God!* He has everything under control. He knows the end of the story. In fact, He wrote it and knows it's a good ending. Is He indifferent to what goes on in this world? Of course not, because He hates to see us hurt ourselves. But God isn't sitting up there with His mind worrying and wondering how it will all turn out in the end.

*God has everything under control.*

Somehow, by an act of His sovereign power that is way above our human understanding, He already has it all worked out. When Jesus finished His work at the cross, the Bible says, "He sat down at the right hand of God" (Hebrews 10:12). Why did He sit down? Because there is nothing left to do. It has all been accomplished in Christ so the only thing left now is for us to enjoy the relationship we have with Him until the time comes when we see Him face to face.

God isn't hard at work in heaven, trying to make sure it all turns out well down here. His focus is on *you* and the relationship you share with Him. He enjoys you and wants you to enjoy Him too. Consider the way His actions and attitude are described in Zephaniah 3:17:

> *The LORD your God is in your midst, a victorious warrior. He will exult over you with joy, He will be quiet in His love, He will rejoice over you with shouts of joy.*

This verse is the source of the title for today's study. The Bible actually teaches here that God is singing and dancing at this very moment. The word *exult* is the Hebrew word which means to twirl in excitement, as in dancing. The verse goes on to say that God will "be quiet in His love," literally meaning that He will renew you in love as He works in your life. Then it says He will "rejoice over you with shouts of joy." The literal translation of that phrase would mean that He acts joyful and sings songs over you.

> God enjoys you and wants you to enjoy Him too.

Can you imagine God singing as He joyfully works in your life to accomplish His purposes for you? That's what the Bible says He is doing at this very moment!

## AN OLD-FASHIONED LOVE SONG

I was teaching from this verse one day when Helena came to me afterward and said, "I was reading that verse not long ago and noticed that it says the Lord sings over us with joy.' 'Lord,' I asked, 'Do you really sing over me? What could you possibly sing about *me?*' "Immediately," she said, "one of my favorite old songs from years gone by popped into my mind, word for word. At first I tried to dismiss it, thinking, 'This *can't* be the Lord.' But the song wouldn't stop, and shortly I knew it was indeed the Lord singing a song to *me.*"

Helena continued, "I heard Him sing to me, 'You are my sunshine, My only sunshine, You make me happy when skies are gray. You'll never know dear, how much I love you. Please don't take my sunshine away!' I realized then" Helena said, "just how much He loves me! To think that I am the sunshine of His life absolutely overwhelmed me!"

Someone might protest, "Why would the Lord sing a song to her like *that* one?" Don't think that the only songs He knows are religious songs. He sang the song to Helena that He knew would thrill her heart. He wasn't singing to Himself, but to her.

What song do you like that God might sing to you?

_____

Remember, God knows your favorite songs too. He knows your favorite places, your favorite everything! His plan is to see to it that you are able to enjoy it all – beginning now and reaching forward beyond this earth-life toward the non-existent boundaries of eternity. Every good thing you enjoy in life is His love song to you.

> *Every good thing you enjoy in life is His love song to you.*

The background music is always there because He is always singing. Do you recognize the tune? Remember, He doesn't only know the religious songs. He knows every song and sings a thousand stanzas to you everyday – in the laughter of children, in the beauty of a sunset, in the music that stirs you, in the flavor of your favorite food, in the intimacy of your marriage. He knows *your* favorite song.

The song of God's love for you resonates through the universe. Jesus said, "he who has ears to hear, let him hear" (Matthew 11:15). Do you hear the tune? Do you recognize Him singing to you?

My favorite place on this earth is the British Virgin Islands. All of the Caribbean is beautiful, but there is something about the beauty of these particular islands that is almost hypnotic to me. As Melanie and I vacationed there one summer, I lay in a hammock at Cane Garden Bay on Tortola, unable to keep my mind on the book I had brought to read. I stared out over the powdery, white sand across the crystal clear, blue water. As I watched sailboats on the horizon, at one point I literally felt a deep sense of joy and prayed, "God this is awesome! You did a great job here!" At that moment, a thought entered my mind as a still, small voice and gently whispered, "This is nothing. Wait until you see the rest I have for you!"

Think about your life for a moment. There have certainly been times in life when God sang His love to you through things you have seen, heard or experienced. Describe a time in your life that you know was God singing His love to you.

Elizabeth Barrett Browning wrote the poem, "Aurora Leigh." Consider the meaning of what she wrote:

_____

_____

_____

*Earth's crammed with heaven,*
*And every common bush afire with God;*
*But only he who sees, takes off his shoes,*
*The rest sit round it and pluck blackberries.*

What does it mean to say that "earth's crammed with heaven?"

_____

_____

What common bushes have you seen afire with God in your life?

_____

What is the contrast she makes in the last two lines of the poem?

_____

_____

The reality is that God does sing to you in everyday life. If you want to move further toward a greater sense of intimacy with Him, it is important to begin to see and hear Him in the day-to-day details. Many Christians see and hear God only through religious things; but if you want to learn to experience Him in a greater way, it will be very helpful for you to begin to look for "his fingerprints" on the situations and circumstances of your daily routine.

God is too big to be contained by religious trappings. The psalmist said that, "The earth is the Lord's and everything in it." The world is His pulpit, from which He declares His love. We can see His face and hear His voice in a thousand places if we have eyes to see and ears to hear.

Your God is singing and dancing over you. He has prepared so much for you. "No eye has seen, no ear has heard, no mind has conceived what God has prepared for those who love Him ~ but God has revealed it to us by His Spirit" (1 Corinthians 2:9-10 NIV). God wants to show you that Spirit-filled living, the grace walk, is nothing less than a perpetual dance with Jesus Christ.

As you end this week of study, pause and reflect on the most meaningful relationships you have had in your lifetime. Can you see ways that God communicated His love to you through those relationships? Think about the relationships you have now. In what ways is He communicating His love and acceptance through you toward the people He has placed into your life?

In the space below, write a prayer to Him, thanking Him for the specific ways that He has shown His love to you through the people and situations you experience in life. Be specific in the things you point out in this prayer.

*Dear Father,*

_____

_____

_____

_____

In Jesus name,

*Amen.*

# LEARN TO LIVE
# FROM YOUR DESIRES
# INSTEAD OF DUTY

# DAY ONE

# Take A Look At Your Heart

We have passed five mile-markers in our journey toward a deeper intimacy with God. I hope that you have received each of these truths, not only into your mind, but also into the experience of your daily living. This week we will consider another of the key elements of enjoying the love relationship you share with your Father.

Let's begin by answering a question: What motivates you to do the things you do in your Christian walk? In other words, why do you do the things you do as a Christian?

_____

Too many Christians live out their daily walk with a sense of duty as their primary motivation. They read their Bibles, pray, attend church, give, share their faith and do all the other things they do as Christians for one main reason ~ they believe it is what they ought to do. They often feel like it's an uphill battle and that they are fighting against the baser desires of their hearts, but they do it anyway because it's the right thing to do.

This approach to the Christian life sounds admirable on the surface, but the fact is that God never intended for us to live a life that honors Him simply because it's what we ought to do. In fact, living that way can't honor Him because it is a legalistic attempt to live the Christian life and God isn't honored by that approach.

Living strictly from a sense of duty will drain the joy of our Christian walk faster than almost anything you can imagine. Nothing kills inspiration quite as effectively as obligation. That's no way to live in any realm of our lifestyle and is especially true when it comes to experiencing God's love in our lives.

Think about the other relationships you have in life. Do you treat your mate with respect? Why? Is it because you ought to or because it's something you want to do? Do you meet the needs of your children? Is it because that's what a parent is supposed to do or because you love your children and want to meet their needs? You understand the point that it isn't duty that moves you to action; it's love. That's how it is with God.

> *Living strictly from a sense of duty will drain the joy of our Christian walk.*

The grace walk is a lifestyle in which we are motivated by a God-given *want-to* as opposed to the coercion of a religious *ought-to*. Based on the answer you gave in the first question asked, which describes you? Do you live your Christian life from a sense of religious duty or is it a real desire to express love to Him?

Many Christians would say the actions of their lives come from a combination of the two. That kind of double-mindedness is the cause for frustration in a person's life. We can't live partly by grace and partly by legalistic effort. It is important to abandon ourselves to grace if we are going to enjoy the freedom and peace it offers.

Jesus said that He came "so that you might have life, and have it to the full" (John 10:10). A full and rewarding life is your birthright as a child of God. In your study this week, it will become abundantly clear that God's highest and best plan for you isn't that you live a Christian lifestyle out of a sense of duty. His desire for you is that you understand how much He loves you and then, as a result of that understanding, you will live in a way that honors Him because it's what you *want to do*.

The door to victorious Christian living swings on this hinge. Whether you do what you do because of legalistic responsibility or because of a living relationship with Christ will make all the difference in your Christian walk. I'm not suggesting that every time you do something, you will find a conscious sense of desire rising up in you, motivating you to do it. What I am saying is that, when we walk in grace, we do the things we do because the deepest desire of our heart is to honor Christ through faith and obedience.

"Obedience" isn't a legalistic word if we properly understand it. The Apostle Paul wrote these words to the Christians at Rome:

*But thanks be to God that though you were slaves of sin, you became obedient from the heart to that form of teaching to which you were committed (6:17).*

Note here that the source of their motivation to be obedient wasn't in the sheer determination of their wills. It wasn't just because they knew in their minds what to do. Fill in the blank: The obedience of these Christians came _____ _____ _____.

That's how your Father intends for you to live ~ from the heart. A heartfelt expression of your faith is the only way to enjoy the abundant life Jesus has given you. The need many Christians have is to see their own heart for what it really is, because most don't even know what's in their heart.

Don't be deceived by faulty teaching you may have heard about your own heart. I used to believe that my heart was evil and that, by Christ's help, I had to constantly battle against the wicked desires of my heart. I had read a Bible verse many times that caused me to believe that was the case. You probably know the text too. A misunderstanding of this verse has caused a lot of trouble for a lot of people. Without looking it up, fill in the words I leave out of the verse below.

> "Obedience" isn't a legalistic word if we properly understand it.

"The heart is _____ above all things and is desperately _____."

You may have heard this verse, taken from Jeremiah 17:9, taught many times. The problem is that many of us heard it taught without "rightly dividing the Word" (see 2 Timothy 2:15). Some have inaccurately handled God's Word by trying to apply that passage to you, a New Testament Christian.

To rightly understand God's Word, we have to put verses we study into their proper context. In this case, to do that will make a huge difference in what you believe about the meaning of Jeremiah 17:9. Consider the following points about the verse and how it relates to your heart:

1. Is the verse in the Old Testament or the New Testament? _____

Don't underestimate the importance of where the verse is located. While it is true that everything in the Bible is written for us, not every verse there is

written directly *to* us. Even the most stubborn legalist will admit this point. Nobody would argue that we should stone rebellious children, although the Old Testament says to do it. (See Deuteronomy 21:18-21) Nobody would suggest that we slaughter and sacrifice animals today, as the law in Leviticus teaches. There is much in the Old Testament that we don't apply to ourselves precisely because it is in the Old Testament. That is the case with Jeremiah 17:9.

2. Read what God told these old covenant believers in Jeremiah 31:31-34 and in Ezekiel 36:26. In the Jeremiah passage, circle the words "I will" each time you see it. (It is there seven times in the New American Standard Version of the Bible.) God said in Jeremiah 31:33 that a day would come when He would write His Law _____ _____ _____.

Do you see the promise of God through Jeremiah to these Old Testament saints that "days are coming" when He was going to change everything by establishing a new covenant with them?

Look at Ezekiel 36:26 and fill in the blanks:

*"Moreover, I will give you a _____ heart and put a _____ spirit within you; and I will _____ the heart of stone from your flesh and _____ _____ a heart of flesh"* (a tender heart).

Read the surrounding verses in the Ezekiel passage, verses 24-31. Count the number of times God says, "I will" in that passage. Notice how He points out that what the people will do is a result of what He does. He is saying to them, "A time will come when you obey me because it is in your heart to do so. I'm going to give you a new heart so that you obey me because of desire, not because you have to do it so that you can keep me happy."

3. Under the old covenant, people had deceitful hearts that were wicked, but you don't live under the old covenant. You live within the benefits of the new covenant. Don't think that Ezekiel 36:26 was given only to the Jews. Paul wrote in Galatians 3:9 that those of us who are believers have received the same blessing.

In Hebrews 8, the Bible quotes the passage from Jeremiah, and then makes an important point in verse thirteen:

*When He said, 'A new covenant' He has made the first obsolete. But whatever is becoming obsolete and growing old is ready to disappear.*

Has the new covenant been established? _____ This verse says that, because of the new covenant, the old covenant has become _____. It has disappeared.

Has God fulfilled His promise to give a new heart to His saints when the new covenant became effective? _____

Are you one of His saints? _____

Do you now have a new heart? _____

If you want to experience deep intimacy with your Father, you must understand and believe this. Your heart isn't wicked and dirty anymore. He has given you a new heart.

We all still have fleshly desires to disobey God at times, but that isn't a true reflection of what is in your heart. It is only a shallow impulse of the flesh. Make no mistake about it ~ your heart is toward God. If it weren't, you wouldn't even care about whether or not you experience intimacy with Him.

Today's study has required you to look a little deeper into God's Word. If what you have seen contradicts what you've always believed about your heart, are you willing to start thinking differently about the matter? Remember that to grow in intimacy with God, we must be willing to shake off the lies we have believed and embrace the truth of God's Word. It should be clear from your study today that you don't have a wicked heart. Your heart is a new one, given to you by your heavenly Father as a part of the new covenant which He has entered into for your benefit and His glory.

> *We all still have fleshly desires to disobey God at times, but that isn't a true reflection of what is in your heart.*

As you end your study today, write in the space below what the false teaching is about the heart of Christians and then write the corresponding truth.

False teaching about our hearts is that _____ _____, but the truth taught in the Bible about it is _____ _____.

*Week Six*

Now, spend a few moments in prayer thanking your heavenly Father for giving you a new heart. Keep doing this each day until this truth renews your mind. You may have believed a lie about your heart for a long time. Don't expect to *feel* like this is true right away. Keep affirming the truth of God's Word about this matter and eventually your feelings will fall in line with the truth.

# Stop Trying To Change Yourself

*I*n yesterday's study, you saw that the Bible teaches you have a new heart. Yours is neither deceitful nor wicked. You live in the New Testament and have been given a heart that is receptive to the things of God and hungry for Him. Do you see that in yourself? Don't make the mistake of thinking of your behavior in order to answer that question. I'm not asking what you do, but what is *in your heart*. Do you see how much you long to experience the life of Christ and to express it in your daily living? That longing comes from God.

To set the pace for today's study, write a short prayer here to your Father telling Him that you have a heartfelt desire to know Him and His ways more intimately

_____

_____

_____

There are two reasons why it is so important to know your own heart. The first is so that you won't be trapped in the prison of constantly analyzing yourself to make sure your heart is in the right place. Again, if it weren't, why would you still be involved in this study after six weeks? Self-absorption is spiritually exhausting, so don't go there.

Another important reason why you need to recognize the purity of your own heart is so that you won't fall into the rut of trying to improve your heart by changing your behavior. That's an old legalistic ploy that goes all the way back to The Garden of Eden. Nobody changes who he is by changing what he does. Change comes from the inside out. It is precisely by knowing who you are that will change what you do.

Consider this question: If your heart is pure, can you trust it? Of course you can. As you delight yourself in the Lord, something happens in your heart. Read this verse and then answer what it is that God gives us as we delight ourselves in Him.

*"Delight yourself in the Lord; and He will give you the desires of our heart."* (Psalm 37:4)

What is it that He gives us as we delight ourselves in Him?

_____

For many years I misunderstood what this verse is saying. I thought it simply promises that God will give me what I want if I delight myself in Him, but it means much more than that. It is saying that He puts the desires of my heart there. As I grow toward greater maturity in grace, He increasingly gives me the wants I have so that my wants and His wants become the same.

> *As you delight yourself in the Lord, something happens in your heart.*

Now, here's the crucial question: Do you *want* to know the Lord intimately and honor Him in all you do? I hope you give the right answer! Of course you do! If you doubt that, it may be because your behavior doesn't always reflect that truth, but that doesn't change the fact that your heart hungers for Him.

The Bible calls King David "a man after God's own heart." (See 1 Samuel 13:14) What does that statement mean? It means that David pursued God. He hungered for Him. If you want to see how much David hungered after God's own heart, read the Psalms. He repeatedly expressed his hunger for the Lord in the psalms he wrote.

However, if we were to judge David's heart by his behavior, we certainly wouldn't come to the conclusion that He was "a man after God's own heart." At times he acted totally the opposite. He acted cowardly at times. He committed adultery. He had a man murdered. The list could continue.

Judging by David's life, we might conclude that sometimes it takes a while for our outer man to catch up with our inner man. Nobody has a perfect track record when it comes to our behavior. If God required a great performance in order to use people, He wouldn't have anybody to use. In Hebrews 11, we have seen the people listed there as saints of great faith. They all blew it at times ~ many of them in a big way.

So you might as well get past the idea that you have to change yourself by improving your behavior before God can work with you to cause you to experience intimacy with Him. He'll start with you right where you are, if you're willing to admit where you are. The reason so many Christians are trapped in a performance-based, compulsively driven religious experience (I can't bring myself to call it a "Christian" experience.) is because they think something is seriously wrong inside them. They are trying to change what they believe is wrong on the inside by changing what they do on the outside.

> *God will start with you right where you are, if you're willing to admit where you are.*

I am convinced that there are people who are going to church, singing in the choir, teaching Bible Study classes, giving their offerings, reading their Bibles, saying prayers, witnessing to their neighbors and even preaching sermons to try to somehow change something they believe is wrong inside them. I know it's true because I did it. Not only did I do it, but as a pastor of local churches for over twenty years, I counseled hundreds of others who did it too.

They are duty-bound to do what they do in hopes that their activity will prove to be the currency to buy what they want from God. Of course, nobody would put it in those terms, but that's the hard, bottom line. What they want more than anything is a sense of peace that everything is spiritually okay and they are right with God. They do what they do because they feel they must, if they are going to make spiritual progress. They don't know there is never a time they aren't right with God. Jesus has seen to that.

Those who think they have to change themselves by getting their religious act together before they can experience intimacy with God need to know two important realities. The first is that none of us can change ourselves. The second is that we don't have to, because by His grace God transforms us.

> The only thing you have to change is your mind.

The focus of this week's study is on how to live from righteous desires instead of religious duty. That won't happen as long as you believe that you have to change your behavior first. The only thing you have to change is your mind.

## WHAT ABOUT REPENTANCE?

One of the horrible distortions of the meaning of repentance that has often been taught is that it denotes the idea of changing our behavior. That is not what the biblical word means. A change of behavior may be the ultimate result, but the word doesn't mean that at all.

In the New Testament, the Greek word for repentance is *metanoia*, which literally means "after one's mind." It comes from a compound word of the preposition *meta* (after) and the verb *noeo* (to understand or think). The word *metanoia* (repentance) combines the meaning of the two words so that the whole compound word means, "to think differently after." The idea is that a person used to think one way, but now after looking at the evidence, has changed her mind and is thinking in a totally different way.

As you have grown in your own grace walk, have you seen the Holy Spirit completely change the way you understand certain aspects of the Christian life? Can you name a few of them?

1. _____

2. _____

3. _____

What about this whole subject of trying to improve yourself so that you can experience a greater sense of intimacy with God? Have you done that? What are some things you've done to try to change yourself for the better?

1. _____

2. _____

3. _____


Here's where the rubber meets the road in your journey toward intimacy with God. Are you willing to repent of the things you are trying to do to change yourself? The great reformer, Martin Luther once said, "Nothing you do helps you spiritually." Have you traveled far enough down the road of rigorous-religious-regiment to see the truth in that statement? If so, pause at this point in your study to consider this prayer of repentance.

*Dear Father,*

*I realize that I need to repent. I have sincerely wanted to experience a sense of intimacy with you, but I've been going about it all-wrong. I've been trying to improve myself by doing all the right things so that I can enjoy my relationship to you more. I know now that none of those things are going to accomplish what I want.*

*Right now, I turn away from the wrong idea that I have to first do something to experience intimacy with you. I know that you have already done it all. So I repent of my independent attempt to accomplish something you've already done. I know that if there's something I still have to do, you didn't do it all. To believe that is an insult to the finished work of the cross. Now I turn to you and you alone.*

*From this point forward, I'm going to look to you in complete dependence and confidence that my awareness of your love will grow as you work in me. Transform me with your truth.*

*In Jesus name,*

*Amen.*


As you come to the end of your study today, consider how what you have learned today fits the theme of this week's study. What does learning to live out of our desires instead of duty have to do with the need to stop trying to change yourself? Reflect on that question and thank God for enabling you to repent today.

# DAY THREE

## Learn To Exchange Must For Trust

*N*ow that you clearly understand there is nothing you need to do to change yourself before you can experience intimacy with God, you are now ready to do some things associated with the Christian's lifestyle experience for the right reasons instead of wrong ones. Today we will consider three activities that are often done out of a sense of duty instead of godly desire. They are Bible reading, prayer and church attendance.

All over the world, Christians are being taught that we *ought* to do these things, but why? Don't all new Christians *want* to read their Bibles? Don't they *want* to pray? Don't they *want* to be with other Christians? Of course they do, until they are ambushed by legalistic teaching that tells them they *must*. Then, the spiritual activities they loved initially are gradually turned into religious responsibilities they come to believe they ought to do. Through the school of hard knocks, they come to understand how trying to keep the letter of the Law kills. (See 2 Corinthians 3:6)

Think about the time when you first trusted Christ. Describe your attitude toward Bible reading, prayer and fellowship with other Christians then.

_____

_____

Did your attitude begin to change over time? If so, how?

_____

_____

If you find it hard to do these things now, it may be because you're living under the demand of a *must-do* mentality instead of the desire that comes from walking in grace. Let's consider these three normal activities of the Christian life and examine the right and wrong way to approach them.

Many of us have viewed the Bible as some sort of instruction manual that teaches us how God wants us to live. If that has been the way you have viewed the Bible, you are in a position to experience the wonderful exchange "from must to trust" when it comes to how you approach your Bible.

God didn't give us the Bible to be an instruction manual. He gave it to us as a love letter with personalized notes to each of us, which can only be seen as the Holy Spirit reveals them to us.

Prayer is a supernatural and mystical action through which God and we whisper tender expressions of love to each other. It's not something we do for a set amount of time each day so that we can check-off a box in our minds that indicates we've done the right thing.

Church life is a kingdom party where we come together and celebrate the unbelievably rich life He has given us at no cost to us whatsoever. It isn't a building we go to with other people. In New Testament times, the church gathered in buildings, in homes, in the marketplace, and other places. We don't go to church. We *are* the church!

Legalistic religion denies all of that and turns God's gifts into our obligations. It strips us of joyful intimacy and has the gall to turn God's grace gifts into religious duty. It causes you to feel like you would if you found out that a neighbor had given your young child a puppy. They might call it a gift, but you're the one who has to take care of it.

> *God didn't give us the Bible to be an instruction manual.*

*Week Six*

Legalism may call things like the Bible, prayer and participation within the body of Christ a gift, but that's as far as it goes. Now you are expected to maintain it. That's the reason so many Christians have become discouraged.

Let's take a look at how performance-based legalism addresses each of these practices:

## READING THE BIBLE

Who wouldn't acknowledge that the Bible is God's revelation to us? God speaks through His written word. Is it unreasonable that He should expect that we must spend time in His word every day? A daily devotional time in God's Word would seem to be a must for sincere Christians.

Are you spending time reading the Bible every day of your life? How much time do you give to the Word of God? Do you hurriedly read a short passage just so you can know you have done your duty for the day or do you commit yourself to the discipline of ongoing Bible study? You must study your Bible if you really want to experience spiritual growth.

Are you motivated right now to read your Bible? Describe how you feel at this very moment:

_____

_____

## PRAYER

Few believers would argue that, at the very least, we must be faithful in prayer. How often must one pray? The Bible says that we must pray without ceasing. Would less than an hour a day qualify as constant prayer? Consider the needs of your family and friends. What about the needs of the world? The needs are great. How much time do you spend praying each day? Don't you think that we must pay the price in prayer if God is going to move in our circumstances?

How are you feeling about your prayer life right now? Are you motivated? Describe your feelings:

_____

_____

## CHURCH LIFE

While many have forsaken the church, most Christians would agree that to be a good Christian a person must attend church faithfully. If a man comes home to his wife most of the time, but spends the night with somebody else now and then, is he considered to be faithful?

Are you faithful in church participation? Everybody knows we must come together with God's people since the Bible says that we are not to forsake the assembling of ourselves together. Attending church isn't an option; it is a must.

How do you feel now?

_____

_____

We *must* read the Bible. We *must* pray. We *must* attend church. How does what I've written about these things affect you? Do you feel edified by what you've just read? Encouraged? Uplifted and motivated to do better?

I doubt it. If so, legalism doesn't offend you at all, which needs to be a wakeup call. Remember that, when I started this section, I asked you to take a look at how *performance-based legalism* addresses each of them.

I intentionally used the word "must" ten times in the description of these three things to illustrate the effect that a performance-based perspective on life in Christ produces. I hope that when you described how you felt

*Week Six*

after reading each of the sections that your answers reflected the fact that legalism causes us to feel beaten down, judged and condemned.

Look up 2 Corinthians 3:7 in your Bible. In that verse, the Apostle Paul said that legalism is a ministry of _____. In what way would you explain the application of that fact?

_____

_____

Look in the same chapter, 2 Corinthians 3 and verse nine. There, Paul goes on to call legalism the ministry of _____. Did you feel that when you were reading the way I said that legalism would address Bible reading, prayer and church life?

Legalism will cause you to feel beaten down, judged and condemned. It takes the gifts that God has given to us and turns them upside down, telling us that those very things are our gifts to God. Enslaved by legalism, we read the Bible for Him. We pray because we think He is pleased by it. We attend church because He wants us to do it.

> Legalism will cause you to feel beaten down, judged and condemned.

Living in the bondage of *must*, we think we are doing God a favor when we do these things. In reality, it is foolishness. It is Christianity turned inside out and made into an empty superstition, born of a belief that is completely out of synch with divine reality.

Aspects of the grace walk that flow naturally from the lifestyle of one who is trusting Christ each day become a millstone around the neck of those who believe they *must* do certain things to maintain a good standing in God's kingdom. I have used Bible reading, prayer and church life as examples because they tend to be primary targets of legalism.

Until we move from a mentality of must to the mindset of trust, we will find that legalism will take what God intends to bring us real pleasure and turn it into nothing more than a religious performance.

As you end your study today, ask yourself to what extent you live under "a sense of must" in your own Christian walk. Spend a few minutes in prayer and appropriate the freedom that is yours in Jesus Christ. Tell Him that you are going to move forward in simple trust in Him and stop running on a legalistic treadmill.

As you exchange the musts of your Christian experience with trusting Him to motivate, guide and empower you in your grace walk each day, you will discover a deeper sense of intimacy with your Father. Living free from internal demands you have wrongly assumed were imposed on you by God, you will now be able to begin to sense His pleasure with you. That pleasure has nothing to do with what you do, but is simply because you are His child. When we really know and believe that, it is surprising to see how we want to do the very things we have been forcing ourselves to do.

*Week Six*

# Don't Let Other People Control You

*I* hope that by now you realize that your heart truly wants to honor Christ in how you live your life each day. Having set aside the list of things you believed you must do to be a good Christian, you understand that because you *are* a godly Christian there are things you will want to do.

It will be important as you go forward to constantly guard against slipping back into the old legalistic ways you might have lived in the past. In the contemporary use of the word, *religion* refers to certain set of behaviors that people do to try to establish a good standing with God and remain there. The flesh loves religion and will gradually pull you right back down into it if you don't stay on guard.

Paul wrote in Galatians 5:1, "It was for freedom that Christ set us free; therefore keep standing firm and do not be subject again to a yoke of slavery." What does that say to you about your own life?

_____

_____

Nowhere will you find yourself to be more vulnerable toward slipping back into slavery than in the areas we considered yesterday. This is especially true since there is an almost nonstop background noise in the modern church telling us how we *must* do these things.

Remember, you aren't doing God any favors by reading the Bible, praying, being involved in church, or anything else you may do in an effort to please Him. It goes without saying that these are an integral part of authentic faith, but once these grace gifts have been baptized into the stagnant waters of dead religion, they lose all life. They no longer have legitimate meaning, neither to the believer nor God.

Reading the Bible is no longer a joy; it's a job. Prayer stops being a romantic conversation and becomes a quiet time that we have to observe like a child who is sent to his room for a time-out. Church involvement becomes nothing more than a weary responsibility or a social event. All Christians instinctively know their life isn't meant to be that way. Most don't know what to do about it though.

For them, driven religious fervor becomes a one-night-stand repeated over and over and over again. There might be a shallow gratification in one-night-stands, but nobody would ever mistake it for genuine intimacy. Our loving God offers much more than that. He wants us to experience and express His life as a natural part of the soothing rhythms of grace. However, to live that way means that we live by intention and stop allowing ourselves to be controlled by the expectations of other people. Sadly religious people are the ones who most often place those expectations on us.

> *You aren't doing God any favors by reading the Bible, praying, being involved in church, or anything else you may do in an effort to please Him.*

Jesus didn't come to help you be a religious superstar. Others may value that, but God doesn't. To experience intimacy with Him may require that you stop your religious frenzy, calm down and smell the roses. God doesn't need for you to break the three-minute mile for Him. He just wants you to enjoy Him, knowing that Christian service will flow from that.

In your very first week of study in this book, you learned the importance of not being so caught up in the busyness or a religious lifestyle that you miss intimacy with your Father. How are you doing in that area now? Have you seen how subtly the flesh tries to pull you back to the place where you substitute religious activity for spiritual intimacy?

*Week Six*

Jesus came to deliver us from all that. Don't forget that even in His day, those who were most offended by Him were the religionists who had built their reputation on their religious performance. Their goal was to keep their golden idols polished to a brighter shine than anybody else by keeping the rules of the road that they insisted had to be kept. Theirs was the road to religion, but you aren't on that road anymore. You have learned that Jesus is The Way, not dead religious performance.

Legalistic religionists fill their display case with the idols that most compliment their own personality and temperament. Then they judge everybody else by whether or not they live up to their own personal standards. To them, people are incidental. What matters is how you are behaving.

## DECIDING TO ACT FREE

There is an important choice you will have to make if you are going to live in the freedom that is rightfully yours in Christ. If you sincerely intend to live based on the desires God has put into your heart instead of living by religious demands, you need to settle this question in your mind: *Are you willing to accept the fact that you aren't going to please everybody?* Think about that question for a moment.

> *Are you willing to accept the fact that you aren't going to please everybody?*

The religious world is filled with hardcore legalists who insist that if a person is really the kind of Christian he should be (according to their opinion), he has to fit into a certain mold. The shape of the mold varies, depending on the doctrinal or denominational standard these self-appointed judges use. Those who don't conform to the expectations of these modern day Pharisees will pay a price.

The Apostle Paul suffered at the hands of religious people because he refused to conform to their religious expectations. Consider the following reasons why Paul was persecuted by the religious leaders of his day:

1. They believed he taught false doctrine. (See Acts 9:20-23)

2. They believed that he was too accepting of others outside their own religious circle. (See Acts 22:21-22)

3. They were angry because he taught and did things that violated their long-held traditions. (See Acts 16:20-21)

How do each of these characteristics apply in terms of how somebody who teaches pure grace today might be persecuted by 21st century religious leaders?

_____

_____

What was Paul's response? He answers in Galatians 1:10 (*The Message*):

*Do you think I speak this strongly in order to manipulate crowds? Or curry favor with God? Or get popular applause? If my goal was popularity, I wouldn't bother being Christ's slave.*

Are you willing to write a similar declaration of freedom to live beyond the control of other people? If so, write it in the following space:

_____

_____

## CONSIDER JESUS

Even Jesus wasn't a good churchman by the standards of the religionists of His day. He didn't live up to what they thought He ought to be. To them, He had no convictions. He appeared to compromise the purity and integrity of their values by doing things like healing people on the Sabbath, by eating with crooks (Publicans) and party animals (sinners) of His day.

Jesus didn't separate Himself far enough from the riffraff, as every good churchman knew everybody should do. Consequently, He lost His testimony with the Pharisees, an incidental matter that didn't seem to bother Him at all. Jesus cared more about relationship than reputation. He still does.

Consider the way Paul described Jesus in Philippians 2:5-7

*Week Six*

*Let this mind be in you, which was also in Christ Jesus; Who, being in the form of God, thought it not robbery to be equal with God, but made himself of no reputation, and took upon him the form of a servant, and was made in the likeness of men (KJV).*

This text says that Jesus was willing to make Himself of no reputation in order to serve mankind by bringing us salvation. In the end, it was the religious leaders who had Him killed. Jesus came into the world "full of grace and truth" (John 1:14) and He was rejected. It may be helpful to recall the words Jesus told His disciples to remember in John 15:20:

> *Jesus was willing to make Himself of no reputation in order to serve mankind by bringing us salvation.*

*Do you remember what I told you? 'A servant is not greater than the master.' Since they persecuted me, naturally they will persecute you. And if they had listened to me, they would listen to you!*

My goal here isn't to create a sense of apprehension in you about what you might experience from other believers as you walk in grace. However, I know that it is important for you to be prepared when religious legalists criticize you for not conforming to what they think you ought to be.

If you are going to move further along in your journey toward intimacy with your Father, it is absolutely necessary that you live in freedom from the need to please other people and be accepted by them. Many religious people didn't accept Paul. The other apostles and disciples weren't accepted either. Even Jesus wasn't. That's important to fully understand because when people begin to see more and more of Christ in you and less and less religious legalism, you can be sure you won't avoid criticism.

The question is, what are you going to do when you are criticized? It comes back to the question I asked you earlier, *Are you willing to accept the fact that you aren't going to please everybody?*

I've known many Christians who have never reveled in the love of God because they can't answer a definite "yes" to that question. They're so busy trying to milk love out of other people through their religious performance that they can't enjoy the unconditional love and acceptance of their heavenly Father. Are you willing to accept His acceptance and be content even if others misunderstand or malign you?

Don't let other people control you. As we end this study time today, write your thoughts about the pressing question of this study. Don't underestimate its seriousness as it relates to the matter of enjoying intimacy with God.

*Are you willing to accept the fact that you aren't going to please everybody?*

_____

_____

_____

_____

# Go With The Flow

As we come to the final study of this week, I hope you have a greater sense of your true self and that you are growing more comfortable with what you know about who you are in Christ. You've seen that you can trust your heart because God has given you a new one that hungers to glorify Him. You have discovered that you are able to live from the godly desires resident inside you instead of by the demands of the religious world around you. You aren't obligated, but are *free* to serve the Lord because that's what you want.

Yesterday, you made peace with the reality that as you walk in grace you won't please everybody. That's okay too because your goal is to please your Father and you now know that you please Him simply because you are His child. When it comes to your daily walk, that won't be hard either considering that He causes His desires to become your desires as you delight yourself in Him. It's beginning to make sense what Jesus meant when He said, "My yoke is easy and my burden is light" (Matthew 11:30). We just focus on Him and He will take care of the details.

## A GENTLY FLOWING RIVER

An authentic Christian lifestyle isn't a flash flood, but a gently flowing river. Jesus said His life would flow out of us like a river of living water coming from our hearts. (See John 7:38) As He flows out of us, we experience Christianity in this world the way God designed.

How do you hope Christ will change your lifestyle in practical ways as a result of what you've studied this week?

_____

_____

People who don't feel fully accepted by God are often driven to do more and more religious things to try to gain His approval. None of that is necessary because He doesn't lead us that way. Instead He has chosen to make us lie down in green pastures. He leads us beside the still waters where He restores our souls.

All we need to do is go with the flow of His life that we possess. We have nothing to prove by the frantic pace of a ministry marathon He never asked us to enter. It isn't possible to hear the still, small voice whisper when we are running at full throttle. God invites you to stop and rest. Get in touch with your heartfelt desires and you will be thrilled to see that they align perfectly with the plan He has for you. You don't have to *make* yourself serve God when you know His love.

The kind of teaching presented in this week's study can be scary to those who have been heavily indoctrinated in a legalistic way of living. They're afraid it leads to stagnation in our spiritual walk. One of the accusations against people who believe in biblical grace is that we think it's not important whether or not we do anything in service. They say we embrace a passive lifestyle where we don't do anything, but sit around waiting for Christ to do it.

> *He leads us beside the still waters where He restores our souls.*

That criticism shows that they don't understand what we really believe. Ours isn't a lifestyle of spiritual laziness hiding behind a misinterpretation of the word "grace." On the other hand, living the way God intends doesn't mean that we have to be working ourselves to death with religious activity either. What it does mean is that we trust Christ and act *as He leads us*. You can be sure that when a Christian knows the love of God he *wants* to do anything and everything that His Father has planned for him.

One part of growing into spiritual maturity is moving beyond the adolescent stage of religious busyness so that we live out of the calm confidence

*Week Six*

of the union we share with God through Jesus Christ. I hope that you will live outside the religious rat race you may have known in the past and let the only race you run be the one that takes you straight to Him.

Being freed from a sense of religious duty, you will find yourself at a place where you can ask yourself what wonderful things God intends to allow you to do with the time you have in this world. By looking into your heart and trusting what you see, you may discover some things you've either never seen before or else afraid to acknowledge are there.

## THE GIFT OF A DIVINE MISSION

One morning I was reading the prayer in John 17 that Jesus prayed on the night before He was to be crucified. He said something in the fourth verse of that chapter that really caught my attention. He said, "I have glorified You on the earth, having accomplished the work which You have given me to do."

As I read that verse, my heart was filled with a desire to be able to say the same thing when I am ready to die. "I have glorified you on the earth, having accomplished the work you have given me to do." Strangely enough, over the weeks that followed, the Lord showed me that the greatest threat to my fulfilling what He has planned for me isn't because I'm *not* doing what He wants me to do. The real threat is getting caught up in doing things He has never called me to do.

*Christian growth is a gradual process where we move forward almost imperceptibly at times.*

Even now, I find myself susceptible to taking on too many things instead of staying focused on the things God has planned for me. Sometimes, when I've allowed myself to be buried by an avalanche of activity, I have told my wife, "I can teach the truth about resting in Christ. I just can't live it!" Of course, that's not true, but it seems that way in my frustration. Do you ever feel that way about your Christian life?

The fact is that old habits die hard. Christian growth is a gradual process where we move forward almost imperceptibly at times. As the old saying goes, "I'm not where I want to be but, thank God, I'm not where I used to be."

It seems like blasphemy to some people to suggest that the need in their lives may be to do less, not more. The just-do-it dogma ranks right up there with the deity of Christ among hyperactive Christians who don't understand waiting on the Lord.

*Journey into Intimacy*

Many people find themselves in a place that can be compared to the man adrift at sea in a life raft. Because he is dying of thirst, he begins to drink the seawater around him. The salt water causes him to become thirstier and his thirst causes him to drink more seawater. This vicious cycle will bring death if he keeps on with it.

This is the fate of the Christian who believes that doing more is the remedy for his thirst. Sometimes the answer to our deepest need is met when we understand that the best way to advance may be to retreat, remember that God's ways aren't our ways. Blase Pascal said, "The sole cause of man's unhappiness is that he does not know how to stay quietly in his room." The bottom line is that it's not frenzy, but faith that leads us to intimacy with God.

I used to say that when it comes to serving Christ, I'd rather burn out than rust out. The fact is, though, either way you are *out*. Your Father has a divine mission in life for you. Don't miss it by allowing yourself to get caught up in a thousand things He never asked or expected you to do.

> *Your Father has a divine mission in life for you.*

The disciples in the upper room cast lots and chose someone to replace Judas when the only thing they had been told to do was wait there. The man they chose is never mentioned again.

Moses sensed God calling him to lead the children of Israel out of Egypt, but jumped the gun by killing a man instead of waiting for God to do it His way. The result was he spent the next forty years tending sheep in a desert.

Abraham fathered a child with a servant girl named Hagar instead of waiting for God to give him the son He had promised. Today the descendents of Ishmael and Isaac are still fighting.

Do you get the picture? God has a plan, but when we take it on ourselves to do things He hasn't asked us to do, all kinds of problems can be the result. Here is the relevant question to consider about your own lifestyle:

What are you wasting time doing that is interfering with your ability to carry out the divine mission that God has for you?

---

The problem with getting sidetracked isn't usually that we're doing bad things with our time. The things we are doing may be good things, but they aren't *God* things. Allowing ourselves to get caught up in all sorts of activities ~ religious or otherwise ~ that we haven't been called to do present several problems. They waste our time. They dilute our energy. They distract our focus. Can you think of others?

On each side of the roadway to intimacy are ditches of dead duty that will cause you to come to a standstill on your journey unless you avoid them. Don't allow yourself to go through the motions of dutiful drudgery you haven't been called to do. Life is short. Let Christ live through you and do what He puts in your heart to do. That's where intimacy lies and where you'll find fulfillment in your lifestyle.

As you end your time of study today, think about the way you live your life. Do you live like a person who is driven? Are you allowing yourself to waste time and energy on things that you don't need to be doing?

The focus of this week's study has been on living out of your desires instead of a sense of duty. Many Christians have never been able to get in touch with their God-given desires because they've always been a slave to doing what they believe they are supposed to do. If that has been your situation, pray and ask your Father to show you how to rearrange your lifestyle.

Write down a few of the things that you believe reflect the God-given desires of our heart:

1._____

2._____

3._____

How do you intend to exercise faith so that these begin to be the focus of your time and energy?

_____

_____

# Week Seven

# OPEN YOUR EYES
# AND SEE

*Journey into Intimacy*

## DAY ONE

### *Look!*

*H*ave you come far enough in your journey toward intimacy with God that you encountered some unexpected scenery along the way? What have you learned or experienced so far that you didn't expect when you started out on this journey?

_____

_____

One sign of growth is change. The only things that don't change are dead things. Living things change over time as they grow. That fact is especially true for you as God is transforming you by His grace so that you will experience a deeper intimacy with Him. Don't ever be unsure about changes you see God bringing to you. If you are growing, you will see a change in the way you understand some things and in the way you live your life. Anybody who tells you that they are the same person now as they were years ago is making a sad confession, whether they know it or not.

Your study this week will be exciting because it will give you an opportunity to grow in the way you experience your Father's life and love. The theme for the week is "Open Your Eyes And See." What you are going to learn to see more clearly through the five studies in this chapter is your

Father's presence in your daily routine. You are going to learn how to hear Him express His love to you more often and in ways that might surprise you. You may discover how to see Him in places you've never thought to look until now.

*Many people just don't have the eyes to see the Lord in daily life.*

The fact is that many people just don't have the eyes to see the Lord in daily life. You aren't one of those people. Your only need is to know where to look, a simple thing to learn. Once you have discovered how to see your Father in the details of life, you will begin to see Him everywhere ~ smiling at you and reminding you of how much He loves you. Don't you think that will increase your sense of intimacy with Him? It most surely will!

In a short paragraph, describe how and where you see God at this point in your life. It may be at church or in the Bible or in your relationship to family or friends. It may be that you see God in other places. Describe it here:

_____

_____

As you move through this week's study, I'm going to encourage you to look in different directions to see the face of your Father. It is possible to see God in any direction you look because the fact is that He is everywhere. Even now as you read this sentence, He is the air you breathe.

Many people have been blinded to the presence of God, even though He is right there with them. Some fail to recognize Him because they haven't been taught how to open their eyes and see. Even biblical characters at times were blind to the presence of Deity as He stood before them.

## THE EMMAUS ROAD

Do you remember the story of the disciples as they walked along the road to Emmaus with Jesus after His resurrection? (If you don't know the story, pause at this point and read it in Luke 24:13-53.) The amazing thing about that story is that these men who had been with Jesus day and night for three years didn't recognize Him as they walked along with Him. Why do you suppose they didn't recognize Jesus?

I think it may be for the same reason many don't see Him even though He is with them today. They weren't expecting to see Him. After all, Jesus had been crucified and buried a few days earlier. We can't fault them for not expecting to see somebody they had watched die and be buried.

We all tend to see what we expect to see. Jesus said, "According to your faith, that's how it will be for you." (See Matthew 9:29) If you don't expect to see Christ manifest Himself to you in your day-to-day living, you probably won't see Him. That doesn't mean He isn't there. It only means that you aren't looking with expectation right now. Maybe it would be a good idea to pause here and ask the Lord to open your eyes so that you will begin to see Him in your daily walk.

> *We all tend to see what we expect to see.*

Write your prayer here:

*Dear Father,*

_____

_____

*Amen*

Those disciples on the Emmaus Road didn't see Jesus because they weren't expecting to see Him, but it will be different for you. As you move further in your grace journey, you will fully expect to see Him and you won't be disappointed.

In John 18:38, at the trial of Jesus, Pilate asked one of the most sad questions a person has ever asked. He said to Jesus, "What is truth?" What's sad about that? The reason it is sad is because of whom He was talking to at the time. There was Jesus ~ *The Truth* ~ standing eighteen inches in front of his face and Pilate didn't know the Truth when he saw it.

On Resurrection Day, Mary was at the tomb of Jesus to mourn His death. She didn't know He had arisen from the grave. When she saw two angels inside the tomb, she started sobbing because the body of Jesus was gone. She asked them where His body had been taken, then John 20:14 tells what happened next:

*When she had said this, she turned around and saw Jesus standing there, and did not know that it was Jesus.*

Why didn't she recognize Jesus? It was for the same reason the disciples on the Emmaus Road hadn't recognized Him. She wasn't expecting to see Him. Are you beginning to see the problem that keeps people who sincerely love Jesus today from seeing Him? Put it in writing here just to confirm that it is clear in your mind:

_____

One more example: Once during a violent storm, as the disciples toiled in windy weather at sea aboard a fishing boat, Jesus came walking toward them on the water. Most cried out when they saw Him, "It is a ghost!" Only one man in that boat had recognized His true identity. (Matthew 14:25-29)

> *Jesus is always here where we are. He never leaves.*

These biblical characters were no different than many today that wish they could see Jesus, while not recognizing His presence among them. Jesus is always *here* where we are. He never leaves. Our Lord is not a theological proposition—He's a Person with thoughts and feelings and desires just like we have. His greatest desire is for us to understand how much He loves us, and to love Him in return. He doesn't just want us to believe He is with us. He wants us to *recognize* Him with us.

## WHY WE DON'T SEE JESUS

We can't afford to be too hard on these biblical characters. After all, if we're honest, we'll admit that far too often we breeze through our day with little more than a few passing thoughts of the Lord, much less enjoying a conscious awareness of His presence. What is it that keeps us from seeing

Him in everyday matters? It has much to do with not understanding how He relates to us.

Many Christians don't recognize Christ's continuous presence with them because of the subtle way He sometimes chooses to relate to us. He doesn't normally approach us in a pushy and intrusive manner. There are those rare occasions when He suddenly overtakes and ravishes a person with His love, as He did with the Apostle Paul on the Damascus Road. (See Acts 9) However, His normal way is to gently whisper to us in a still, small voice with the goal of drawing our attention and devotion toward Him until we become so totally consumed with Him that, by comparison, everything else becomes unimportant.

For instance, after He had walked the seven-mile trip with the disciples on the Road to Emmaus, Jesus "acted as though He were going further" (Luke 23:28). Why did He do that? Like you, Jesus wants to be wanted by those He loves. Intimacy with Him is the result of an *invitation*, not an *intrusion*.

> *Intimacy with Jesus is the result of an invitation, not an intrusion.*

The disciples *urged* Him – "Stay with us," they insisted. (Luke 23:29) So He did. This is so typical of the way Jesus behaves. First, He attracts us to Himself until we long to know Him more intimately, then He reveals Himself to us more and more as we respond to the level of knowledge we already have of Him.

There is another reason we often can't see Jesus with us. It is because we get so bogged down in our personal lives. It's easy to become so preoccupied with our own circumstances that it seems Jesus gets lost in the shuffle. The disciples walking the Emmaus Road with Christ were bogged down in their despair about His crucifixion. At the moment Jesus came near them, all they could see were their seemingly adverse circumstances.

To call them shortsighted is an understatement. They could only see the superficial—the natural elements—and thus, were blind to the supernatural of the moment. They were interpreting life through a human paradigm that made no room for the possibility of a divine breakthrough into their situation.

Have you fallen into that same mindset in your own Christian journey? If you want to experience a deeper sense of intimacy with Christ, can you see

how that it is important that your eyes be opened so that you can see Him with you?

As we end this session today, why don't you pray and ask the Lord to open your eyes so that you will begin to see Him in your daily life. He opened the eyes of the disciples on the Road To Emmaus and He will do the same thing for you. He wants you to enjoy intimacy with Him at every moment in your life. He doesn't live at your church. He lives inside you and wants the two of you to share your life together every day.

What is it that has distracted you from the awareness of His presence with you at every moment? Ask the Holy Spirit to show you and then ask Him to put those things in their proper perspective in your life so that you won't be blinded to the presence of Jesus with you.

Spend some time praying about this now, and then go out into your day with your eyes wide open, expecting to see Him. Look! As your vision improves over the coming days, you most assuredly will begin to see what you are looking to see!

# DAY TWO

## *Look Outside*

Do you want to grow? Remember that we have established that the only things that don't grow are dead things. So here's a question you have to consider: How will you grow if you keep believing and doing nothing more than the same old things you've believed and done all along?

The fact is, sometimes we reach a place in life where something needs to change. That doesn't mean that we necessarily need to abandon our past ways of doing things. It might just mean that we need to expand in the way we function, adding to our past.

It is probably a safe generalization to say that most Christians have tried to relate to God primarily through religious means ~ you know, church services, Bible studies, sermons, books and songs written by Christians ~ that sort of thing. Don't think for a minute I plan to criticize those things. In fact, I fit in that category as a Christian author.

What I am going to suggest is that we limit ourselves by trying to experience intimacy with God only through churchy type things. Maybe an example from my own life will help make my point clear.

As I've previously mentioned, Melanie and I have loved the chance to occasionally vacation in the Caribbean. At times I have stood in scenic spots overlooking the ocean, with my camera in hand. I've felt overwhelmed by the majestic beauty that surrounds me. Blue, crystal clear water stretches out to the horizon until it becomes impossible to tell where the water stops and the sky begins. White, powdery beaches reach as far in both directions as the eye can see. Picturesque palm trees lean forward with fronds reaching out to the water as if they too desperately want to feel the lapping waves. A gentle breeze that seems to promise to breathe youth into any person who will inhale its ocean fragrance. Do you have the sense of what I'm describing?

Now, imagine at those moments that I lift a fifteen-dollar disposable camera to my face so that I can take a picture and capture the beauty that lies before and around me. I don't want to lose this moment. I love it and I want to seize it on film. I want to pull the total impact of everything I'm experiencing at the moment through that camera's lens and take it home with me on a 3x5 photograph. I want to go home, look at this picture and feel exactly what I'm feeling as I stand on the beach at that moment.

*Jesus is the personification of God's love—a love much too big to be contained by religion.*

Do you think it will happen? Of course not. A snapshot could never do justice to the beauty. It's only a minuscule representation of what I've seen, but it just can't do it justice. It can only remind me of the beauty of the moment, it can't duplicate it. The beauty is simply bigger than any camera can capture.

That's how it is when we try to see the beauty of Jesus only through a religious lens. He is the personification of God's love—a love much too big to be contained by religion— consequently He reveals Himself in religious *and* nonreligious ways. For instance, the Bible says that, "The heavens declare the glory of God" (Psalm 19:1). Clouds aren't churchy. The blue sky isn't religious. So God doesn't only communicate through church-talk, but also through cloud-talk. These are only two of His many dialects.

What I pray happens in you as you study this week is that you will begin to recognize new ways to see your Father's face outside the religious ways you may have experienced Him in the past. Think about it for a minute. What are some ways a Christian might see God that aren't religious?

_____

_____

Maybe it seems odd that I would suggest that looking for the presence of Jesus with a religious perspective can hide Him from us, but that's often the case. There are certainly ways in which we can see Christ within a context often classified as religious. Again, in no way would I want to diminish the value of the ways that Christians traditionally have sought to experience the Lord's presence in their lives. I'm not suggesting the Lord doesn't make Himself known to us in these ways, but rather that traditional religious means aren't the *only* way that Christ manifests Himself to those He loves.

Those who only expect to see Him within a religious context greatly limit their ability to recognize Him. They are looking for Him through a lens with the diameter of a straw when, in reality, He is showing Himself to us in a panoramic view that encompasses all of life.

*Those who only expect to see Him within a religious context greatly limit their ability to recognize Him.*

## SEEING HIM IN NATURE

Today's topic is called "Look Outside" for two reasons. The first it to challenge you to look outside the walls of the church to see your Father. The other is to challenge you to literally look *outside*, to meet your Father in nature.

Have you ever experienced intimacy with your Father through nature? It is a fulfilling experience to meet Him there. The Bible repeatedly shows how we can hear God in the still quietness of nature. Consider this verse from the Psalms and write down what it means in the space provided.

"The voice of the Lord is upon the waters" (Psalm 29:3).

_____

"The heavens are telling of the glory of God; And their expanse is declaring the work of His hands. Day to day pours forth speech, And night to night reveals knowledge" (Psalm 19:1-2). What does this verse tell you about God revealing Himself through nature?

_____

*Week Seven*

Isaiah said that "the mountains and the hills will break forth into shouts of joy before you, and all the trees of the field will clap *their* hands" (Isaiah 55:12, NAS).

I once heard a professor ask his class, "Do you *really* believe the Bible? Have you ever seen a mountain sing or a tree clap its hands?" While his question stemmed from cynicism, it's a good question. Have *you* seen a mountain singing or a tree clapping? You can, because nature does indeed resound with the voice of God and show us His face ... if we develop the habit of looking and listening.

The professor's problem was that he didn't understand how God uses mountains and trees and everything else in nature to sing. He thought in terms of listening with one's *physical* ears and to do that, nobody would ever hear it. It's like trying to hear an FM radio station when all you have is an AM receiver. Just because you don't hear it doesn't mean it isn't being played! The problem is that you aren't tuned in to the right frequency.

We've all heard the perplexing question, "If a tree falls in the forest and there's nobody there to hear it, does it make a sound?" But let's recast that question this way: If the mountains sing and the trees clap their hands to declare the presence of God...and nobody listens, does that mean the mountains' melody and the trees' joyful applause stop?

> God's voice continues through nature whether we listen or not.

*No!* God's voice continues through nature whether we listen or not. The difference is that when we don't have hears to hear, we lose. We miss out on a divinely appointed provision for more intimacy with Him. We miss out on hearing His love for us resounding through His creation.

Have you heard the Divine Lover sing to you in quietness of nature? In modern society where people often don't venture outside the concrete jungle, there is a faint song in the distance, inviting those with ears to hear to "come apart and rest awhile." That faint song is for you.

Do you sense an inner stirring to withdraw from the busy demands of life and meet Jesus Christ in a quiet place? There may be protests in your mind about responsibilities and schedules, but does your *heart* hear the Divine invitation? If time were no problem, is the thought of aloneness with Jesus in nature appealing? If so, you can be assured that you're hearing the gentle voice of your Divine Lover inviting you to come away with Him for a while.

Don't allow your head to beat your heart into submission. Follow your heart. You can trust it; remember? In fact, the Bible says that out of it come the issues of life. (See Proverbs 4:23)

Quiet retreats alone in nature have the capacity to bring profound change to your life. After you have been alone with Christ in this kind of setting on a number of occasions, you'll find that you begin to hunger for it. In reality, what you are experiencing is the indwelling Christ within you desiring time alone with *you*. It's *His* hunger for you that you're sensing.

*Quiet retreats alone in nature have the capacity to bring profound change to your life.*

When you do become aware of it, you'll find that you begin to hunger to be alone with Him too. That's the way it is with lovers, even when one of them is God. It's His way of extending an invitation to you to come away with Him to a place where you and He can sing the songs of your heart to each other.

If you want to move forward in your journey toward a greater experience of intimacy with God, it will help you to be open to new ways of experiencing God. Realize that He may show Himself to you in ways that are new to you. Don't rule out getting alone with Him in nature as a great way to cultivate a deeper sense of intimacy with Him.

# DAY THREE

# Look Inside

Yesterday we considered the idea of looking outside at the beauty of nature around us and seeing our Father's presence in that beauty. If you haven't had the chance to find a solitary place in nature yet, I want to encourage you one more time to do that. I hope you won't dismiss yesterday's study as the bias of an author who happens to be a nature-lover.

Many people have agreed that, alone with their Father in nature, they sensed His love in an unusual way. There is a reason church retreats are often scheduled in beautiful natural settings. It's because when we get away from it all and go to a beautiful place in nature, the environment is conducive to experiencing God. The same is true if it's just one person. If you can't get to the beach or mountains or lake, many state parks have beautiful areas where you can be by yourself with the Lord. Try it and see if you don't find it to be spiritually refreshing.

Today, we are going to look in a different direction. Instead of looking outward, I'm going to ask you to look inward where you can experience the conscious love of Christ through prayer. In beginning this section, I thought about suggesting that prayer is looking upward, but then decided to approach it as being an inward look since that is where He lives.

Intimacy with our Father in prayer is strengthened when we realize that God isn't out there in heaven, bending over to hear us when we speak to Him. At salvation, His Spirit came into you and has taken up permanent residence. (See John 14:16) If you want to find God, you don't have to look far. There is never a moment of your life that He isn't with you, closer than your next breath. Read the following verses and describe where God is in relationship to you at this very moment:

Hebrews 13:5 "I will never desert you nor will I forsake you."

_____

1 Corinthians 6:17 "But the one who joins himself to the Lord is one spirit with Him."

_____

John 14:20 "And in that day you will know that I am in my Father, and you in Me, and I in you."

_____

Jesus Christ isn't just with you; He is *in* you and has no plans to go anywhere else! Understanding the union you share with Him will move you further toward experiencing a deeper sense of intimacy with Him.

He knows you completely and still loves and adores you. Growing in intimacy with God requires us to look inward and, through prayer, open ourselves completely to Him. By believing that you are completely accepted by God just as you are, it empowers you to be vulnerable and totally honest with Him. As we submit our inner lives to Christ, we will become more and more aware of His love for us. The awareness of His love will become the motivation and enablement for us to live a lifestyle that is befitting a godly Christian.

> *He knows you completely and still loves and adores you.*

What motivated the Apostle Paul to serve Christ?

_____

Was your answer "his love for Christ?" Read this verse and see what Paul says about the matter:

*"For the love of Christ controls us" (2 Corinthians 5:14).*

Notice that Paul did not say that it was love *for* Christ that controlled him. He said it was the love *of* Christ. I like the way *The Message* puts it: " Christ's love has moved me to such extremes. His love has the first and last word in everything we do."

The motivating force in Paul's life was Christ's love for him, not his love for Christ. Of course Paul loved Christ just as we do, but "we love, because He first loved us" (1 John 4:19).

> *The motivating force in Paul's life was Christ's love for him, not his love for Christ.*

Do you want to see your prayer life be radically strengthened? It can happen if you see prayer as a means for experiencing His love for you. We have all learned the rote characteristics of traditional prayer. You know ~ praise, petition, intercession, etc. I'm not suggesting that these don't have their place, but when we turn prayer into a rote routine that we go through in the same way we perform other duties that we know are good for us, prayer loses its significance in our lives. That's why so many Christians find it hard to maintain a consistent prayer life. They have turned it into a legalistic spiritual exercise instead of enjoying it for what it is ~ a time of intimate interaction with a Divine Lover who adores us.

Describe what your prayer life looks like at this point in your life:

_____

_____

Did your answer include anything about experiencing your Father's love through prayer? Since by nature God *is* love, doesn't it seem logical that when He interacts with us as we pray He would want to express that love to us?

The story is told of a peasant who every day after work would stop by his village church on the way home. He would leave his pick-ax and spade outside and enter into the church, where he sat in silence for about an hour. Then he would stand up, leave the church and continue on his way home.

The village priest had watched this man from the back of the church. There was nothing apparent in the old man's actions that gave a clue to why he was there or what was going on within him. Puzzled by the strange habit, he one day decided to approach the man and ask about his practice.

"Why do you come into my church day after day, old man?" the priest asked. "And why do you waste your time doing nothing when you are here?"

The old man looked at him.

"Sir," he said humbly, "I simply look at Him and He looks at me, and we tell each other that we love each other."

Prayer may encompass more than that, but without this component to prayer, it easily becomes a monotonous duty. If you have been programmed to think of prayer as a set time you talk to God that has to include certain religious elements in order to be valid, it may be necessary for the Holy Spirit to renew your mind on the subject.

*To experience intimacy with God in prayer requires that we understand the basis of grace-based prayer.*

To experience intimacy with God in prayer requires that we understand the basis of grace-based prayer. I'm not going to give you a how-to list about prayer. Instead, I am going to give you a foundational truth about what it means to pray in grace. You will discover that when you fully understand and believe this, it will motivate you to pray because you *want* to and not because you think it's your duty.

## PRAYING IN GRACE MEANS WE CAN TAKE HIS LOVE AS A GIVEN

The worm theology that many of us learned which stressed how bad we are has put a damper on many people's prayer lives. You aren't a dirty sinner who has to come before God groveling and begging. You have been given a new identity. You are now completely righteous (Romans 5:17), holy (1 Corinthians 3:16-17), a divine work of art (Ephesians 2:10), a person who is 100% accepted because you are in Jesus Christ (Ephesians 1:6). Because of Jesus, we can "come boldly to the throne of grace" (Hebrews 4:16).

If you have a habit of groveling before God about what a horrible person you are, stop it. You have been made clean by the finished work of

*Week Seven*

the cross. It may seem humble to speak of yourself in disparaging terms, but in reality it insults the finished work of the cross. Christ has transformed you. Don't talk like that fact isn't true.

Do you remember the vision Peter had in Acts 10:10-16 about the animals that were lowered down on a sheet? God told Peter to eat, but he protested because there were animals there that were considered unclean by Jews. Peter told the Lord, "By no means, Lord, for I have never eaten any-thing unholy and unclean" (10:14). Look in your Bible at verse sixteen in that chapter. God told Peter:

*What I have cleaned, don't you call* _____.

What God has cleansed, we should never call unclean. What He has made holy we should never call unholy. Since He has done both to you, does it make sense to pray and tell God that we don't believe He has done what He said? That's exactly what we're doing if we put ourselves down in prayer while God considers us a work of art created by Him.

It's a terrible and binding error to ever think that when you pray, God is frowning at you. *He is not.* God *loves* you and nothing you have done or ever could do is going to change His mind about you. His loving thoughts are always toward you. Theologian Angelus Silesius astutely observed in the 15th century, "If God stopped thinking of me, He would cease to exist." It's God's nature to continuously think of you and His are always loving thoughts.

*God loves you and nothing you have done or ever could do is going to change His mind about you.*

To move further down the road toward a deeper intimacy with your Father, it is important to have the right attitude when you pray. Come before Him joyfully and with confidence, not with an attitude of doubt about His love and denial about who you really are. Many a Christian has believed they were acting humbly, when what they were really doing was rejecting God's Word. If you want to talk about who and what you are when you pray, affirm the truth not lies about yourself!

Let's end our study today with an imaginary exercise. Picture this in your mind:

*Imagine Jesus walking into the room where you are right now. He walks across the room and stands directly in front of you. He reaches out and puts His arms around you, and pulls you close to Himself to hug you.*

*Relax.*

*Still your busy mind.*

*Just rest in His embrace.*

*He gently presses His face against your own and quietly whispers in your ear, "I love you so much. Do you know how proud I am of you? I love you more than you can possibly know. Sh-h-h. Be still and know that I love you."*

*Listen to Him.*

*Wait until you sense an inner calmness.*

*Ask Him to speak a personal word, just to you.*

Listen.

*Do you hear His voice?*

*Linger here, in this still, quiet place, and allow Him to express His love.*

*Wait until you know it is appropriate to resume normal activity.*

*Revel in His love.*

*Don't rush this exercise.*

Are you uncomfortable with such an exercise as the one described in the preceding paragraphs? Is there anything unbiblical about what I've described? Is there anything untrue about the above scenario?

Sometimes when I teach this material, somebody suggests that this exercise sounds "too New-Agey" for them. I know New Agers use visualization. That's not what I'm asking you to do here. I'm simply using a word picture to help you connect to the love Jesus has for you. Jesus *does* love you just as I have described. He *does* embrace you in His arms and longs to express His love to you in meaningful ways. I haven't asked you to visualize anything that isn't biblically true. I just want you to use your faith to see in your mind's eye something that is very real.

As you grow into a stronger grace-based prayer life, you will discover a deeper sense of intimacy with your Father. A legalistic prayer life is hard to

*Week Seven*

maintain, but when we understand that prayer is intended to exist in a climate of total acceptance and unconditional love, our prayer lives will come alive.

As you end your time of study today, I encourage you to take a few minutes to pray. Spend some time thanking your Father for how much He loves you. Thank Him for transforming you by taking you out of the kingdom of darkness and bringing you into His kingdom of light.

# DAY FOUR

## *Look Around*

$\mathcal{A}$s you are moving through this week's study, is the Holy Spirit opening your eyes so that you are seeing Christ in a clearer way? I hope that as you have looked outside the walls of religion and as you've looked inside through prayer to the Christ who indwells you that your sense of intimacy with Him is growing.

Today, I am going to ask you to "look around." As I've previously mentioned, the whole world is God's pulpit. He isn't locked up in a church building waiting for you to come there so that He can reveal Himself to you. He wants you to see Him in a multitude of things in daily life.

God doesn't stand outside world culture, refusing to interact with it. To the contrary, He is very much involved in the details of culture and can use cultural elements to make Himself known to those who have eyes to see. Have you ever seen God revealing Himself to you in the nonreligious aspects of culture? Are there things you enjoy that nobody would call religious, but you know you have experienced an awareness of your Father through those things? What are a few of the nonreligious ways you have encountered God in your life?

_____

_____

Today I ask you to consider some of the more common cultural elements of our society as a medium through which the Lord can reveal himself to you. To suggest that God can speak to you through aspects of modern culture doesn't minimize the place of the Bible. God will never speak in a way that contradicts His Word, but He certainly speaks in ways apart from the Bible.

God has often spoken to people through things directly created by Him. He can make Himself known through thunder (1 Samuel 7:10); through lightning (Isaiah 29:6); through fire (Exodus 13:21); through a bush (Exodus 3:2); through the skies and land (Psalm 19:1); even through a talking donkey (Numbers 22:28). The list could go on and on.

> *God has often spoken to people through things directly created by Him.*

In addition to those things created directly by Him, He speaks to us through the creativity of others too. The word "creativity" finds its root in the word "create," which means "to bring into existence something out of nothing." The ability to create always finds its ultimate source in God, for He alone is the Creator of all things.

Created things (such as human beings) can't create, unless they are *endowed* with creative ability. Like everything else vested in man from the beginning, our ability to create has been contaminated by sin, but the ability is, nonetheless, of divine origin. Any talent to create you or I have been given isn't something that we can boast in. Our creative abilities are imperfect reflections of His *perfect* creativity.

Our Father's creative ability can be seen through human creativity and in many of the things we create. Sometimes He shows up the most unexpected places, secretly smiling at those who have eyes to see Him through the elements of our culture.

## SURPRISE! IT'S ME!

Shortly after I was married, my parents and younger sister moved out of the country for five years because of my dad's work responsibilities. I only saw them once during that five-year period. I was nineteen when they left and I deeply missed my family. I looked forward to seeing them more than words could express.

When the time drew near for their return to the states, my dad arrived a few days ahead of my mom and sister, unbeknownst to me. I had been out to lunch and as I pulled into the parking lot of the church where I was serving as pastor, I saw my dad sitting in his car. But because I wasn't expecting to see him, I didn't recognize him. In fact, I didn't really pay him any attention. I casually glanced at him and parked my car.

When I began to walk toward the building, my dad spoke. "Hey there, young man," he said. Instantly, I recognized his voice. I whirled around and ran toward him. It was one of the great thrills in my life and I'm sure that my dad enjoyed the pleasure of suddenly surprising me with his presence.

That's how Jesus Christ acts toward you. In some ways, there are times when He wears the icons of our culture like a disguise. He hides Himself from the world – from those who don't want to see Him—but at unexpected moments He suddenly pulls down the mask and gives those He loves a clear glimpse of His face. At those moments, those who love Him squeal with excitement, "Jesus, it's *you*! I see *you* in that!" I have no doubt that when this happens, He laughs with delight.

Are you open to having the Holy Spirit expand your understanding of how to see your Father in the ordinary, everyday icons of life? You will be thrilled when He enables you to look beyond the superficial and see the supernatural. Jesus is waiting to surprise you with His presence. Open your eyes to see Him in the everyday icons of culture.

> *Jesus is waiting to surprise you with His presence.*

What are these cultural icons? They are the common expressions of human creativity seen in our society. As examples, let's consider two of the "secular" symbols of our society that have the potential to become sacred ground when we recognize Jesus in the midst of them.

## HEARING CHRIST IN MUSIC

No medium on earth has the capacity to affect a person's emotions like music. Music has been used throughout history to move people into action. It has motivated men to charge forward into battle. It has often been a prerequisite to making love. Music has caused some to sit in reflective silence and caused others to get up and dance. It has soothed fussy babies until they drifted off into a peaceful sleep. It has been used at weddings to celebrate a new life together and years later at funerals to grieve the end of that shared life. Music has been a comforting companion to prisoners and slaves. It has given expression to a celebration of victory. Certain music has even been

*Week Seven*

proven to increase the amount of milk a cow gives! Music – it can make us laugh or cry. It can give us feelings of nostalgia, joy, hope, sadness and even anger. Its power is nothing short of miraculous.

Have you encountered Jesus through music? What are a few songs through which He has spoken to you?

_____

_____

Certain songs move me deeply, causing me to experience a sense of intimacy with my Father in awesome ways. I seldom hear or sing *The Love of God*, *Great Is Thy Faithfulness*, or *A Mighty Fortress Is Our God* without choking up. The great hymns of the faith can often teach us theology far better than any sermon and at the same time touch us in the deep places of our heart.

*The power of music is nothing short of miraculous.*

Don't make the mistake of thinking that you can only hear your Father's voice within the context of religious music. Remember, He can make Himself known to you in unlimited ways. He isn't about to surrender everything outside the church doors to the world. Music written apart from His life is pirated material and our God can reclaim it anytime He wants.

I was speaking on this subject at a conference one day when I asked the group, "Are you able to hear God speak to you if there is no religious tone to what you hear?" The audience waited for me to continue. "Close your eyes and listen to the song I'm about to play, " I encouraged them. "Perhaps you have heard the song before, but this time, listen for the voice of the Divine Lover in it."

Then, at a spiritual retreat, in a room filled with Christians, I played a recording of an old song by the famous classic rock singer, Joe Cocker. The words he passionately sang are, "You are so beautiful to me. You are *so* beautiful to me. Can't you see? You're everything I hoped for. You're everything I need. You are so beautiful to me!"

As the song played, grown men and women began to cry. For the first time, many were hearing the voice of the Divine Lover from a source they had never thought to consider before now. For every person there, this song would never again be the same. God's love had redeemed it and brought it into the kingdom as a gift for those who *listened*.

Does this concept seem uncomfortable to you? If so, consider this question: Why should Jesus Christ be restricted to only communicating to you in religious ways? He *is* Lord over all the earth and can use anything He chooses to express love to those who are His! One unmarried lady I know says that she listens to a radio station that plays nothing but romantic love songs and that she often hears the Lord sing to her through those songs. Who would tell her she is wrong?

I have experienced a sense of transcendent joy that couldn't possibly find its origin in fallen man at times when I have heard certain non-religious music. I was enthralled as I watched a live performance of the musical *The Phantom of the Opera*. On another occasion, tears filled my eyes as I attended a concert by the great Italian singer, Andrae Boccelli, despite the fact that not one word was being sung in English. I could almost imagine Jesus saying, "Isn't this great? Steve, I love seeing how you enjoy this concert. I can't wait until you get Home. I have even better ones waiting for you here."

Don't misunderstand me. I'm not suggesting that every time we have a positive feeling, it's God manifesting Himself to us. I recognize that our emotions can be manipulated by various influences. However, I also believe that Christians are sometimes guilty of dismissing the pervasive presence of Christ in this world by insisting that experiences that aren't directly religious are non-spiritual or even evil.

Think about some songs you like that aren't religious. Is it possible that you could hear your Father's voice in any of them? Pick one and write the words in this space:

_____

_____

_____

> *He is Lord over all the earth and can use anything He chooses to express love to those who are His!*

## JESUS AT THE MOVIES

Some Christians renounce movies as "from the devil." *Hollywood* is snarled from the lips of some believers as if to say it leaves the taste of bile in their mouths. "Can anything good come out of Hollywood?" they ask.

There is no question that, as is true with music, there are some abominable productions being made today. But are we to completely dismiss films as being an arena outside the realm where God can work and speak? Can and will our Father reveal Himself to us through this particular cultural icon? I believe that He will.

I admit that I'm a movie buff. My wife tells me that I can get a sermon out of any movie. I don't watch movies looking for spiritual applications. I just see them. I have left many movies, having seen the face of my Father smiling at me between the scenes, whispering secrets between the actor's lines. Maybe others in the theater didn't see Him, but I know what I saw.

> *Can and will our Father reveal Himself to us through movies?*

In the movie *Chocolat*, I saw the power of authentic grace over religious legalism. In *Les Miserable*, I became teary watching the effect that unconditional love and forgiveness can have on a person, as depicted by the life of Jean Valjean. In *The Legend Of Baggar Vance*, Will Smith's character reminded me that I already have everything I need in Christ. All I need to do is find my "authentic swing" by trusting in what He has already given me by His life. The list of movies could continue. Many have been platforms through which I unexpectedly heard the voice and saw the face of God. I know Jesus goes to the movies. I've seen Him there.

As you watch contemporary films, open your mind to the fact that the movie might be a parable for you. Jesus used parables (basically fictional stories) to explain spiritual realities when He taught His disciples. He will do the same thing today as He teaches you more about His life, His grace and His love. This is seeing God through the creative gift He has given others.

It isn't necessary to sit down to watch a movie, *trying* to find something "spiritual" in it. Just relax and enjoy the show. He will reveal Himself to you more and more as you learn to be open to divine whispers in the ordinary places of life.

Think about some of the movies you have enjoyed. Great stories endure through the years because they speak to us on a deep level. They involve those who need to be rescued in some way, antagonists who threaten to destroy the innocents, a hero with redemptive ability who comes to the rescue, and they usually end with a union of love that lasts happily every after. Have you seen these elements in the great films you have enjoyed? Look at these elements again and you'll see that they are the same matrix on which the gospel story stands.

Think about your favorite movies. Think about the storyline of each film. List the spiritual applications that could be made if you were to view the movies as parables. Consider the following questions as you recall each movie:

*Films are one way to recognize your Father's presence in everyday life.*

- Was there a message about love in the movie? If so, what was the message and how can it relate to my relationship to my Divine Lover?

- What was the conflict in the movie? As a parable, what can this movie say to me about the appropriate way to resolve conflict in my own life?

- What characteristics of God could I learn about from this movie? His sovereignty? His love? His patience? His goodness?

Films are certainly one way to recognize your Father's presence in everyday life. There are, of course, many other cultural elements through which you can see Him. Great novels can often reveal spiritual truth in a way more powerfully than non-fiction. Art has always been an iconic expression that has often shown us our Father's love. Poetry, dance, sculpture—or even the more common creative efforts such as sewing, cooking, woodworking ... the list of ways God can be seen through creativity goes on and on. By understanding that He speaks through creativity, the Holy Spirit will be able to teach you how to hear His unassuming voice within the culture of your routine lifestyle.

Ancient believers said that we live in a "God-bathed world." They meant that God can be seen everywhere if we just look. Do you believe that?

If you want to experience a deeper sense of intimacy with God, I encourage you not to rule out the possibility of seeing Him in the world around you. To look for Him only through a religious lens is like trying to perceive the world by looking through a straw. Open your eyes and see that He is all around you. Begin to look and you might find Him smiling at you in places that surprise you.

As you end your study today, think about the ways you might experience your Father's love by looking around at contemporary culture. Ask Him to make you more sensitive to the times and places where you can see Him.

# DAY FIVE

## *Look Far*

During your study this week, you have been challenged to look in various directions so that you can experience a greater sense of your Father's love. You have looked outside to God's creation to see evidence of His love there. You have looked inside yourself to the Christ who lives in you and found that He loves you so much that He is one with you, guiding your life, not because of how much you love Him but because of how much He loves you. Yesterday, you were challenged to look around and see Him giving you glimpses of grace in icons of culture where many would never think to look for Him.

The topic of today's study is "Look Far," meaning that in order to grow in intimacy with our Father, sometimes we have to look beyond this world. We have to look toward eternity where God's eternal purposes are being carried out exactly according to plan. The reason we need to "look far" is because there are times in life that if we were to judge God's love for us by what we can see right under our noses, we would find it hard to believe He loves us as much as we've been told.

It seems much easier to believe God loves us when everything is going well in life, but what do we do when life seems to be unraveling around us and we can't see God's hand anywhere in our disastrous situation? We look far, focusing our attention on what is eternal instead of allowing our hope to be destroyed by circumstances we experience in our short time on this planet.

We have all faced times when we've been tempted to question God's love for us because things were so hard at the time. Either you have experienced that in your own life or you may even be experiencing it now. In the space below, identify the situation that caused you to question God's love:

_____

_____

There is never a time when we are more vulnerable to believing the lies of the enemy that when we are going through terrible trials. It is at those times that what you have come to believe about your Father in the past will either make or break you. If you have already established a strong foundation of faith in Him, you will blindly cling to Him even when you can't see any logic in what He is allowing. If you enter your disastrous darkness without a settled confidence in His goodness, you will find yourself susceptible to the lies that are whispered to you from out of the darkness. That's why it is so important to settle in your mind that God is good. The time will come when your confidence in that fact will be the only thing that sustains you.

> *It is important to settle in your mind that God is good.*

## A DISCIPLE NAMED JOHN

Most people believe that the John who wrote the gospel by that name and the John who wrote The Revelation are the same person. When he wrote the last book of the Bible, John had been exiled there because of his testimony for Christ. Patmos was intended to be a prison to him, where he would live out his days in a lonely, barren land. Imagine being abandoned on an isolated island and left there alone. To say it would be a place where a person could become discouraged and depressed would be an understatement.

Apparently John didn't see Patmos as a dead end to ministry, but as a curve in the road. While he was there, he had a vision of end times that is amazing. God gave him a panoramic view of the divine plans for the universe. What kind of man was this, who was able to "look far" beyond his immediate circumstances and see the eternal realm to the point that he got a glimpse of God's eternal plans?

Rather than immediately give you the answer, I want you to discover it for yourself. In the gospel John wrote, he is identified the same way in five different verses. Look up these verses in your Bible and read them: John 13:23, 19:26, 20:2, 21:7, and 21:20. Each time John is mentioned in these verses, he is called the same thing. What is it? "The disciple whom Jesus _____."

I used to wonder why the Bible referred to John that way, but didn't refer to the other disciples with the same description. Then one day it hit me ~ *John* wrote the book! He called *himself* "the disciple whom Jesus loved." That wasn't a nickname he picked up from others. He gave that name to himself! What a great way for a follower of Jesus to see himself and identify himself to others.

If you were to write a letter and identify yourself based on how you have found God to be in your own experience, what would you write?

_____

_____

Some might identify themselves as "the disciple whom Jesus healed" or "the disciple whom Jesus set free from drugs" or "the disciple whom Jesus miraculously gave a clear conscience" or countless other ways to describe ourselves. John saw himself primarily in terms of being loved by Jesus. I think I like that one best, don't you? It encompasses everything we need from our Father. If He truly loves us, then everything is going to be okay regardless of what comes our way.

That was how John described himself as he thought about the time he spent with Jesus. It was years after writing his gospel before he wrote the book of the Revelation. The reason this is important is because I want you to see the point I made earlier. John didn't wait until he got to Patmos to decide what he believed about his relationship to Jesus. By the time he was exiled, he had settled a long time ago that he was loved.

> *If He truly loves us, then everything is going to be okay regardless of what comes our way.*

Have you settled this in no uncertain terms in your own life? If so, write a prayer below, thanking your Father for the fact that you are greatly loved by Him.

*Week Seven*

*Dear Father,*

_____

_____

_____

*Amen*

If you want to continue to experience a sense of intimacy with God when you are going through great trials, you'd better settle this matter in your mind now. God loves you. Hold onto that truth because it isn't impossible for a Christian to find himself at a place in life where that's all he has.

## OPEN YOUR EYES AND TAKE THE FAR LOOK

There was John on a deserted island when one day he heard the voice of God: "Come up here , and I will show you what must take place after these things" (Revelation 4:1). Note what the Bible says happened next:

*Immediately I was in the Spirit; and behold, a throne was standing in heaven, and One [was] sitting on the throne (4:2).*

The Holy Spirit called John to enter in through this door and to see beyond the natural world into an eternal world. His body was on Patmos, but, for a time, he was able to see beyond the bounds of his physical location and see his spiritual home. John saw that he was actually living in two worlds at the same time – the physical and the spiritual.

As a Christian, you too live in dual worlds. If you want to experience intimacy with God regardless of what you may go through in life, it is imperative to look beyond the physical world and recognize that there's another dimension where you also live. There is another reality to our lives beyond what we can see—and we live in that world, really.

John wasn't the only one who got this point. The Apostle Paul wrote in 2 Corinthians 4:18, "While we look not at the things which are seen, but at the things which are not seen; for the things which are seen are temporal, but the things which are not seen are eternal." Paul said the same thing as John – you live in a world you can't see with your eyes.

Not only do you live in a dual world – physical and spiritual – but the spiritual world is the *dominant* world. It's within this dominant world that believers find our real home. Your residence in this physical world is only temporary. So when you are going through hard times and hunger to experience intimacy with God, take the long look! Look far beyond the troubles you face at the moment and realize that you are a citizen of another world. The short-term trials of this life won't last forever, but heaven will and, thank God, there will be no trials there!

> *Your residence in this physical world is only temporary.*

The devil will try to rob you of your sense of intimacy with God by shifting your focus away from eternal reality and cause you to stare at the troubles right under your nose. Don't fall for it! Keep looking at Jesus. When John looked through that open doorway between earth and heaven, he saw a throne and Somebody was sitting on it! Don't forget ~ that Somebody is in complete control of every detail in your life!

Sometimes what needs to change is our focus. If we open our eyes and see the far look, we will discover that God is on our side and has everything worked out already. One example of this is found in the Old Testament, in 2 Kings 6:8-17. Eugene Peterson recounts the story well in *The Message*:

"One time when the king of Aram was at war with Israel, after consulting with his officers, he said, "At such and such a place I want an ambush set." The Holy Man sent a message to the king of Israel: "Watch out when you're passing this place, because Aram has set an ambush there."

So the king of Israel sent word concerning the place of which the Holy Man had warned him. This kind of thing happened all the time. The king of Aram was furious over all this. He called his officers together and said, "Tell me, who is leaking information to the king of Israel? Who is the spy in our ranks?" But one of his men said, No, my master, dear king. It's not any of us. It's Elisha the prophet in Israel. He tells the king of Israel everything you say, even when you whisper it in your bedroom.

The king said, "Go and find out where he is. I'll send someone and capture him."

The report came back, "He's in Dothan." Then he dispatched horses and chariots, an impressive fighting force. They came by night and surrounded the city. Early in the morning a servant of the Holy Man got up and went out. Surprise! Horses and chariots surrounding the city! The young man exclaimed, "Oh, master! What shall we do?"

He said, "don't worry about it – there are more on our side than on their side."

Then Elisha prayed, "O GOD, open his eyes and let him see." The eyes of the young man were opened and he saw. A wonder! The whole mountainside full of horses and chariots of fire surrounding Elisha!"

This story is a perfect example of the connection between our focus and our consciousness of our Father's protective love. When the servant of Elisha could see only the physical world, panic struck him and contentment disappeared instantly. Elisha, however, wasn't focused on the temporal, but looked beyond the door and saw the eternal, where everything was under control.

So it is with you. Your life is hidden with God in Christ. Your roots are in heaven, even as you read this. Your contentment comes from that life, not this one. If you want to experience intimacy in the midst of your trials, look beyond what you can see in the natural world and, by faith, see the truth as it exists in the supernatural world.

*If you want to experience intimacy in the midst of your trials, look beyond what you can see in the natural world.*

As you end your study for this week, exercise your faith to open your eyes and see your Father's love everywhere in life. Don't let the problems of this temporary world rob you of the awareness of your Father's lavishing love for you.

In the space below, write a description of your circumstance and how it's affecting your life. Does your current focus cause you to interpret the circumstance by what you can see in this world or are you looking "through the open doorway" into the spiritual world?

Slowly read 2 Kings 6:8-17 again and ask the Holy Spirit to personalize the passage to your own life situation. Are you Elisha or the servant? Pray before you close this book today and ask that your eyes will be opened and that you will *see.*

# Week Eight

# LET LOVE BE YOUR TRADEMARK

## DAY ONE

# Keep Standing In The Truth

Here we are, coming to the end of our eight-week journey together. I hope you have taken ownership of the seven truths we have seen as we've moved forward. The key to continuing to grow in intimacy with your Father is to keep renewing your mind with what you have learned during these eight weeks.

Many believers grew up with wrong ideas about God, themselves and what it means to live the Christian life. We are all held back from enjoying intimacy with our Father in direct proportion to the extent we hold onto faulty beliefs. Remember, knowing the truth sets you free, but believing lies has the opposite effect. That's why it's so important that as you end this study you continue to renew your mind with truth that will reinforce what you've learned.

Just as there is healthy food and junk food at the grocery store, there are materials available to Christians that can help and materials that can hurt you spiritually. Don't believe everything you hear or read. Live as a discerning Christian.

When Luke wrote about the ministry of Paul in Berea, he commended the Christians there for something they did when they heard the Bible taught. Here's how he described them in Acts 17:11:

*Now these were more noble-minded than those in Thessalonica, for they received the word with great eagerness, examining the Scriptures daily to see whether these things were so.*

These Christians were hungry for the word, but they didn't automatically swallow everything they were fed. They checked it out to see if it was true. How did they do that?

By examining the _____ to see whether _____ _____ _____ _____.

As we mature in grace, we learn to be discerning about what we do and don't accept as truth. In no area of our belief system is that more important than what we believe about God. The word *theology* literally means "a word about God (*theos* and *logos*)."

> As we mature in grace, we learn to be discerning about what we do and don't accept as truth.

What is your theology? In other words, what do you have to say about God? Has your view changed any since you began this study?

Imagine giving a description of what God is like to somebody who had never heard of Him. How would you describe Him to them in a short summary? Write your description:

_____

_____

_____

I hope you mentioned God's love in your description. Since that is the essence of His nature, to do justice to any description of Him requires that we talk about His love. If the world only understood the truth about the love of our Father, so many more would come to Him in faith. Sadly, their understanding is often a distorted caricature of who He really is.

One reason it is so important to understand and accept your Father's love is because we all eventually become like the whatever we imagine God to be. People trapped in legalism see God as a judgmental, cosmic eye-in-the-sky who is watching and waiting for them to mess up in the way they live. They imagine that how they behave is what matters most to Him. Consequently, that's the kind of person they become in the way they relate to other people. They become harsh parents, demanding friends, dictator-type pastors, etc.

What they need is to understand the *agape* love of their Father. That's where you come into the picture. As a grace-walking evangelist, you will become more and more effective in sharing His love with others as you become more and more persuaded of how much He loves you. You won't have to struggle to witness, but will *be* a witness because you can do no less than point people to Him through your walk and your words.

Jesus Christ is head over heels in love with you. Have you become fully persuaded of that truth? He plans to spend eternity proving His love to you in ways beyond your wildest dreams. His love is pure, yet passionate. It is an objective fact with profound subjective implications for your life. He longs for you to know how much He loves you, to *feel* how much He loves you and to see how much He loves you.

> *Jesus Christ is head over heels in love with you.*

As the revelation of God's extravagant love becomes more and more real to us, love becomes our trademark, our identifying characteristic. It's what we're known for, just like love is what God is known for too. More will be said as you move through this week's studies about sharing God's love. For now, make a mental note that as you experience deeper intimacy with Him, you will become more and more like your Father. The outcome of that is that you will find yourself becoming more loving to everybody.

If others were to describe the kind of person you are right now, what would they say? Would they use the word "loving" in their description? What one word would each of these people use to describe you?

Your mate? _____        Your children? _____

Your best friend? _____        Your co-workers? _____

People at church? _____        Your neighbors? _____

Don't condemn yourself if you can't imagine some of these people using the word "loving" to describe you. Transformation is gradual, but it will come to you as you continue to grow in intimacy with God.

As you experience your Father's love, you will begin to express it more and more to other people. Some people you encounter won't immediately accept it though. Be prepared that some will resist because it doesn't make sense to them.

Some will caution you against the dangers of shallow emotionalism. That viewpoint isn't totally wrong. There are those who reduce their understanding of the relationship they have to Christ to the place of emotionalism. Nobody would deny that, *but* there is an equal or maybe even greater danger that many people will spend the rest of their lives relating to God only through their minds. Religious intellectualism is just as far out of bounds as shallow emotionalism.

The idea of *unconditional* love from God is hard for some people. They will ask questions like:

*What if I turned my back on God and renounced Him?*

*What if I intentionally committed a horrible sin?*

*What if I am spiritually lukewarm?*

*What if I lose faith?*

*What if...?*

There are a thousand "what-ifs" people can ask as they struggle with the idea of unconditional love. The reason they have such a hard time believing that *nothing* can stop God from loving them is because it isn't normal. In fact, it's not even human. It is divine. Unconditional love is rarely seen in this world. Sadly, that's true even among Christians. If you doubt it, just watch what often happens when a Christian falls into sin.

That's why it is so important for you to determine to cling to the truth of God's love. Don't back down on your belief about it for anything. It is the only thing in existence that cannot fail you. "Love never fails," said Paul in that famous love chapter in 1 Corinthians 13 and it is the truth.

Stand strong in the truth about God's unconditional love. In time, you will become known for it. It will become your trademark, not a bad way to be known!

As you end your study today, ask the Lord to empower you not to compromise what you know is true about His love. Cling to it until you are known for it!

*Journey into Intimacy*

## Don't Ever Forget How Special You Are

*I*t is an amazing thing to consider that you are special to God. Don't you agree? One of the important aspects of experiencing intimacy with Him is to see ourselves the way He sees us. We've already discussed in a previous week's study what a horrible mistake it is to put ourselves down while calling it "humility." I hope you have said a loud "AMEN!" to that as evidenced by how it changed the way you talk about yourself. If God calls you special, who are you to disagree?

What makes you special? Him. He has transformed you by His grace and made you into a wonderful person. I'm not writing this to pump you up with a positive self-image. My prayer is that you have a *biblical* self-image. This verse has been mentioned before, but take a close look at it now:

*For we are His workmanship, created in Christ Jesus for good works, which God prepared beforehand so that we would walk in them (Ephesians 2:10).*

What does it mean to say that we are God's *workmanship*? The Greek word is the word *poiema*. Do you see any other familiar English word embedded within *poiema*? The word "poem" is clearly recognizable there. The Greek word literally points to something that God made with His own hand.

*Week Eight*

## GOD DON'T MAKE NO JUNK

Think about the things God has made. When the Bible describes the creation story, it tells us His response to the things He made. Genesis 1 gives an overview of the creative acts of God, and then the chapter ends with a notable statement. Look up the last verse of Genesis chapter one in your Bible and fill in the blank in this verse:

*"God saw all that He had made, and behold, it was _____*
*_____."*

Ethel Waters was the featured soloist in Billy Graham Crusades for many years. Her mother was a rape victim and Ethel was born as a result of that incident. Before becoming a Christian she carved out a notable place for herself in theatre and film as a pioneer for African-American actresses. She used to share her life story in the Billy Graham Crusades and, when she told about how she had been conceived, she would conclude by saying, "I know I'm somebody 'cause God don't make no junk."

> *If you feel like a dirty sinner, guess what you'll be inclined to act like.*

While her grammar may have been off, her theology was right on target. Everything that God makes is very good. He "don't make no junk." Do you believe that you are one of the *very good* works of God?

The reason this is so important is because if a person has a spiritual inferiority complex, his feelings will never align with the truth and the sad reality is that many people's actions are driven by what they feel. If you feel like a dirty sinner, guess what you'll be inclined to act like. Feelings have a strong influence over what we end up believing unless we intentionally embrace and affirm truth until our feelings change. That's what I'm asking you to do about the truth that you are special to your Father.

## DISCOVERING OUR VALUE

Do you want to see how special you are to your Father? Consider this verse in the Bible. Jesus said:

*The kingdom of heaven is like a treasure hidden in the field, which a man found and hid again; and from joy over it he goes and sells all that he has and buys that field (Matthew 13:44).*

Answer these questions about that scenario:

1. What is the hidden treasure? _____

2. Who sells what he has and buys the field? _____

For many years, I thought that the treasure in this story is Jesus. My viewpoint was that gaining Him is worth giving up everything in this life. I believed the story suggested that we should be willing to turn to Him, regardless of the cost. After all, I reasoned, it will be worth it!

I hope you didn't answer that way because nothing could be further from the truth. The treasure isn't Jesus. The treasure is *you*! You might feel some internal resistance to my suggestion of such a thing, but it's true. You are the treasure. The field in this example is the world (see Matthew 13:38) and the one who is overcome with joy about owning this treasure is Jesus.

> The Bible plainly says that, "you have been bought with a price."

How can we be sure about this? Because the treasure *was paid for* by the one who received it. That means the treasure couldn't possibly be Jesus. You didn't buy Him; He bought you! The Bible plainly says that, "you have been bought with a price" (1 Corinthians 6:20).

It's amazing how we tend to want to make everything be about ourselves. We interpret Scripture so that we come out on top in the story. For instance, how many times have you heard The Story of the Good Samaritan told with the application being made that we are to be the Good Samaritan? The fact is that story teaches no such thing. Our role in that story was that of the man lying on the ground, wounded and bleeding. The Good Samaritan is Jesus. The law and prophets saw us lying there and knew our condition, but didn't solve our problem. They could diagnose it, but they couldn't help it. Jesus did. We didn't come along and find Him. He found us and saved us from certain death.

One more example ~ back to Matthew 13. Look at verses 45-46:

*Again, the kingdom of heaven is like a merchant seeking fine pearls, and upon finding one pearl of great value, he went and sold all that he had and bought it.*

By now I expect you are wising up to this, but I'll have you answer these questions to be sure:

1. Who is the merchant? _____

2. What is the pearl of great price? _____

I'm sure you've gotten it by now. How often have you heard Jesus called "The Pearl of Great Price?" Sermons have been preached for centuries on that subject. "Could all those preachers in the past be wrong?" somebody might ask. Yes. Don't think that because somebody lived a long time ago, that gave him the edge on being right. Don't assume that something right can be determined just because a majority agrees about it either. Remember, it was a majority who screamed, "Crucify! Crucify!" on a fateful day long ago.

Of course it isn't Jesus, but *you* who are the pearl of great price. What great price did we pay for Jesus? None! He, on the other hand, has paid the ultimate price with the sacrifice of Himself. "Jesus paid it all. All to Him I owe!" Remember?

> *You are the pearl of great price.*

I realize that looking at these passages this way may be different from the way you've seen them in the past, but can you see that it has to be this way? We can't interpret these verses in a way that makes us be the hero who finds Jesus and buys Him. You know that's not right. He found us. He paid everything so that He could have us. He wanted us so badly that the price was not too high to Him. Nobody took His life from Him. He willingly laid it down for the world. He bought the field so that He could have you!

Do you see how special you are to your Father? He gave everything to have you as His own. If you want to stay on the road of intimacy with Him, you must never forget how special you are.

Most Christians have gone a long time without feeling special to God. They've been beaten up and put down by religion, by self-condemnation, by recognition of their less than perfect performance and a hundred other things. Beginning to feel special to our Father isn't something that happens instantly. The Psalmist said, "He restores my soul" and that's what it is ~ a restoration process. It takes time.

On of the things that greatly helps move the process along is to keep affirming the truth about the matter. As you end today's study, I encourage you to take a little extra time to do two things. First, take your Bible and see if you can find other verses that tell you how special you are to Him. Then, spend time praying and talking to your Father about what you've learned today. Thank Him for paying the ultimate price for you. Praise Him for the fact that He considers you a precious treasure to Him. Affirm to Him that you believe what He has said about you in His Word, even though your feelings may not connect to the truth about the matter yet.

Finally, in the space below, write a declaration of faith about who you are to your Father. Specifically write about what He has done to make you His own. Write about what changes He has made in your life since He bought you. Don't promise anything. Don't write about what you plan to do. Write only about what He has done and is doing in you. That way He gets all the glory.

# DAY THREE

## Share the Love

Many have described the essence of intimacy as "into-me-see," the idea being that people who become intimate come to know each other at deep levels that aren't seen in shallow relationships. I've seen that proven most in my marriage. Melanie and I certainly seem to see into each other. We married two months after she graduated from high school. It would be fairly accurate to say that we've practically grown up together

There's something we experience at times that could almost make me believe in Extra Sensory Perception if I didn't have a more reasonable answer for it. Sometimes we think the exact same thing at the exact time. One of us may say something that we aren't even remotely talking about and the other will say, "I was thinking that exact thing." It's uncanny.

As I've said, I might tend to think those moments are an experience of ESP, but I don't think that's it at all. I believe that my wife and I know each other so well that we've come to the place where, in many ways, our thought processes run on the same track. In other words, we think alike. Something subliminal may trigger a thought in her and in me at the same time. At those moments, it seems like we're reading each other's minds. The reality, though, is better than that. Over the years, we've grown together and see the increasing awareness of our oneness in deepening ways as time goes by.

That is exactly what happens as the level of intimacy we have with our Father grows. We find ourselves thinking more and more like Him.

Increasingly, we act like Him because we are becoming more like Him with every day that passes. We even start looking at other people like He does.

We start to discover that this intimacy we share with Him begins to spill over into our relationships and attitudes toward them. We reach a place where, without any conscious effort, we begin to bring the presence of Christ into our environment in ways that have transforming power.

Describe your understanding of what it looks like when a Christian brings Christ into his environment in a noticeable way:

_____

_____

_____

There might be many evidences that Christ is showing Himself to other people through you, but there is one that will *always* be present. In a word, it is *love*. You have already studied that God doesn't just love. He *is* love. (See 1 John 4:8)

Whatever else might be seen in your lifestyle, as you begin to think and act more and more like your Father, love will be front and center in your life. The theme for this final week's study is "Let Love Be Your Trademark." We have focused on this matter of allowing Christ's love to flow out of us already, but I want to spend these last few days of your study reinforcing and expanding this thought.

> *This intimacy we share with Him begins to spill over into our relationships and attitudes toward them.*

To the extent we experience the intimate love of the Father, we will be released to pour out agape on others. If we don't know and accept how much He loves us, we will be handicapped in our ability to love other people. John said it like this:

*"We love because He first loved us" (1 John 4:19).*

The only reason we love Christ is because He first loved us. Our love is a response to Him. He is the initiator. But this doesn't only apply to our love for Him. It applies to our love for everybody. As you experience a deepening intimacy with Him, you will find that you begin to love people in a way that isn't natural, but supernatural.

You'll know it's supernatural because the love that comes from God isn't like normal human love. There are several Greek words for love used in the Bible, but the kind of love that comes from God is above them all.

His love is greater than the *phileo* brotherly love known by members of the same family. It's not like the *eros* of passionate love shared between a man and a woman being swept along by raging hormones. It far surpasses the *storge* love that suggests a warm relationship between two people who are completely familiar and comfortable with each other. These are good, but they are human love.

> *The love that comes from God isn't like normal human love.*

God's love is in a class of its own. It is *agape* love. It is an unconditional love that can only come from Him. It is a love that can *never* change because unlike other types of love, it doesn't come forward because of something we see in somebody else. Human love can go away if the things we find loveable about a person go away. Divine, agape love isn't like that. It is a God-love that exists, not because of goodness in the one being loved, but in the one who loves. It comes from out of God's goodness alone. It won't stop because of what somebody may do or not do because it didn't *start* for those reasons.

Think about the people in your life. Who are the ones you can truly say you love unconditionally at this point in your life?

_____

What you're going to find is that, as you grow in intimacy with your Father, your list is going to expand...greatly. "For God so loved _____ _____." Don't underestimate how long your list could become in time.

The Bible says that you have received the divine nature of God. (See 2 Peter 1:4) For that reason, to love people unconditionally is completely consistent with who you are. It's amazing to consider the things Christians are known for these days. If you were to ask the average person on the street, "What are the main things Christians are known for?" what do you think they would say?

_____

_____

Let's go back two thousand years and see what Jesus said about the subject. Here's what He said in John 13:25:

*By this all men will know that you are My disciples, if you have love for one another.*

There may be many things that people today would suggest characterizes Christians, but Jesus said the thing that tells the story is love. If you have the spiritual DNA of Jesus Christ and His is the same as His Father's DNA, and if the very essence of God is love...you get the point. It isn't hard to connect the dots here. It's your nature to love. It's that simple.

What would you say is the focus of your church?

_____

> *It's your nature to love. It's that simple.*

Many churches focus more on how to live than on how to love. The lifeblood of an authentic New Testament church must be sharing the love of God through Christ with each other and with the world. Otherwise, it is nothing more than a religious club.

On the night Jesus was betrayed by Judas, he prayed these words to His Father:

*The glory which You have given Me I have given to them, that they may be as one, just as We are one; I in them and You in Me, that they may be perfected in unity, so that the world may know that You sent Me, and loved them, even as You have loved Me (John 17:22-23).*

Jesus said that He wanted His disciples to go out into the world and show them two things. The first was that God had indeed sent Him. There was something else He wanted His church to show the world. Look at the verse and fill in blank in this statement: Jesus wanted the world to know that God had sent Him because He _____ them.

*Week Eight*

Here's how *The Message* says it:

"Then they'll be mature in this oneness and give the godless world evidence that you've sent me and loved them in the same way you've loved me."

How can we give this godless world evidence of the love of God? By loving them! Jesus asked His Father to cause those who believe in Him to give the world we live in evidence that the same love God has for Jesus is inside us. Our goal is to reveal that love to them too. *That* is our mission in this world, given to us by Jesus Christ Himself. What a great mission we have been given! To reveal the love of God to the whole world is anything but a burden to those of us who have experienced intimacy with Him ourselves!

As you end your study today, think about the unconditional love that your Father has for you. Ask Him to change the way you may look at some people and cause you to begin to love them unconditionally. As you pray, ask Him to show you at least one person to whom you can reach out and show His love in a specific way.

Who is that person? _____

Can you see how that as we reach this point in our journey into intimacy with God, we come to realize that it's not only about our Father and us? We'll look into that topic tomorrow.

# Become A Grace Walker

At this point in your journey into intimacy with your Father, I hope you have begun to experience a transformation in the way you see many things in your life. We never reach our destination in this journey because our infinite God's love has no limits. We will spend eternity exploring the depths of His love for us.

In yesterday's study, we saw that one aspect of our journey down the road to intimacy with our Father is that we find ourselves growing increasingly in love, not just toward God but toward everybody. "Makes me love everybody" said the old spiritual.

Today I want to discuss the three phases of growth in intimacy with your Father. The Apostle Peter said to, "grow in grace and in the knowledge of our Lord Jesus Christ" (2 Peter 3:18). All of us are at a particular place on this growth continuum. As you go through the study today, you will see where you are in your own spiritual development.

## 1. The Grace Crawler

The most elementary level of a Christian's life is the baby Christian stage ~ the crawlers in the church. Babies view the world around them based on how it affects them. To a baby, it's all about *me*. Others have importance to the extent that they are able to meet *my* wants and needs. His perspective could be described as one where it is *Christ and others for me*.

Knowing that he has been forgiven, a new Christian wants to be with other people who know what he knows and have experienced what he has experienced. There's nothing like finding out that there are others who are equally as excited about as he is! He gathers with other people to worship because he wants to be there. He can't wait to get there and goes fully expecting to be blessed. Seldom is he disappointed. His heart is stirred as he meets people who encourage him in his faith.

He is thrilled about all that Christ has done *for him*. He is greatly encouraged by the blessing that other Christians provide *for him* as he connects to them. To the baby Christian, life couldn't get any better.

> *Every Christian is a baby Christian at some point.*

Don't think for an instant that there is anything wrong with this phase. Every Christian is a baby Christian at some point. In the space below, write some other characteristics of baby Christians not mentioned here.

_____

_____

Then the time comes in our grace crawler stage when we start to grow and our focus changes. Crawlers mature into toddlers. At that point, it stops being about "me."

## 2. The Grace Toddlers

As a Christian matures beyond the place of spiritual infancy, he begins to recognize that while we are most certainly beneficiaries of God's grace, the focal point of salvation isn't about us. He will begin to realize that what God does is for His own glory. Christianity is *Christ-ianity*.

As he moves to this toddler stage, the Christian begins to understand that his life isn't about him after all. It is about Christ. This step forward is a big one. It is the time when a Christian starts to understand that the essence of life is Jesus, not himself.

He also begins to realize that the church isn't there to bless him. Along with other Christians, he is there for Christ ~ to glorify Him. At that point, we are still being blessed by God and by other people, but the toddler knows that isn't what it's all about anymore. At that point, our understanding matures to the place where we stop thinking it is *Christ and others for me* and we begin to realize that it is *others and me for Christ*.

Have you reached the place in your Christian walk where you realize it isn't about you, but Christ? I used to think that a good worship service was one where I received a blessing. Then the day came when I found myself wanting to *be* a blessing to the God who saved me.

How would you describe your own experience in this phase of your spiritual growth?

_____

_____

Even this phase of growth isn't the level of full maturity. You might wonder how we could move beyond the place where it is all about Jesus. The answer lies in understanding our union with Him, as we studied yesterday when we examined what Jesus had to say in John 17. The focus of our faith is always Jesus, but as we grow in intimacy with Him we mature into the third phase that God has planned for us.

> *The focus of our faith is always Jesus.*

## 3. The Grace Walker

The third phase of our maturity is where we understand *Christ and me for others*. At this point we come to understand the ultimate privilege of being in Christ. That privilege is to see Jesus Christ express Himself through us in love toward other people. It is Christ taking on our personality, attitudes, attitudes, and actions and expressing Himself through us in a way that people clearly see God's love.

The Bible says it like this in 1 John 4:17: "As He is, so are we in this world." That's it! As He is, *so are we* in this world. When we advance from being a toddler to becoming a mature grace-walker, our lifestyles find their expression in Christ in the way a glove finds its expression by the hand that fills it. If a woman wearing a glove picks up her purse, what picked up her purse ~ her glove or her hand? The answer is "yes" They function as one. The life of the glove *is* the hand.

That's how it is when God's grace empowers us and His love controls our actions. It is you, but it isn't you. It's Christ in you, as you, through you, loving other people. Consider the way the Apostle Paul described in Galatians 2:20. Read the verse, and then rewrite it in your own words.

*"I have been crucified with Christ; and it is no longer I who live, but Christ lives in me; and the life which I now live in the flesh I live by faith in the Son of God, who loved me and gave Himself up for me."*

_____

_____

"It is Christ doing it all through me," Paul said. "As He is, so are we in this world." Does that mean that we *are* Christ like some in the New Age Movement teach? Of course not. That kind of teaching is heresy. What I am saying is that there is a level of maturity that will cause a person to function as a "co-laborer together with Christ" and not just as a servant. (See 1 Corinthians 3:9)

> *There is a level of maturity that will cause a person to function as a "co-laborer together with Christ."*

You have been equipped to "do all things through Christ who [lives inside you] and strengthens you." I once read a sermon by an old African-American preacher, who said, "One day a crippled man was sitting by the gate of the temple when *along came Jesus all dressed up as Peter and John.*" What a great description! Do you get it? As you grow in maturity, it's time to stop begging and start behaving like Jesus is all dressed up in you! We have everything we need in Him. Let's just start acting like who we are ~ containers and conduits of Divine Life.

You have come eight weeks into a journey toward deeper intimacy with your heavenly Father. Knowing what it is to experience His love, don't you find yourself sensing an increasing desire to share that love with others? The emphasis in the church world on the *command* to evangelize becomes a non-issue when we have been deeply touched by the love of Christ. The early disciples of the church said, "we cannot stop speaking about what we have seen and heard" (Acts 4:20).

Nobody has to shame or scold us into caring about people. We can't help but care. We love because He loves us with such intensity that we can't keep it to ourselves. We don't *want* to keep it to ourselves! Because we have experienced His transforming love, we now want to express it. Like Jesus, we want to make the love of the Father known to the whole world. We don't want to be simply religious in the way we do it. In fact, those of us who have experienced real intimacy with God find ourselves loving others to such an extent that it seems radical to a religious mind.

As you finish your study today, go back to the verse we've considered today in 1 John 4:17. "As He is, so are we in this world." Reflect on what that verse means. It obviously doesn't mean we become Jesus. On the other hand, it tells us something about behaving a certain way in the situations of life. Settle in your mind what the verse says to you, and then ask your Father to show you moments today that you can bring His divine life to bear on situations you may face.

# DAY FIVE

## Join The Revolution

*A*s we come to the end our journey together through this book, I remind you that it isn't really the end of the journey. Your journey into intimacy with your Father will never end. In fact, you will discover that the further you go down the road of life in Christ the more beautiful the scenery becomes. He will keep on revealing more and more of Himself to you as you keep pursuing Him with all your heart.

My life was transformed in 1990 when I began to understand my identity in Christ and what it means to walk in grace. (You can read my personal story in my first book, *Grace Walk*.) Since that time, I've seen hills and valleys as I've traveled this road toward a deeper intimacy with my Father. Over the years, I've invited others to take the trip with me and have heard the stories of many whose lives have been transformed as a result.

Has your life been impacted over the past eight weeks as you have studied this book and pursued deeper intimacy with your Father? Describe what changes you've seen:

_____

_____

_____

As we've been discussing in this week's study, intimacy with God isn't something that cuts us off from the rest of the world. To the contrary, experiencing His love releases us on the world as excited evangelists who bring good news of grace to those who are worn down either by their sins or their dead religion.

I've shared God's grace with people on six continents. As I travel around the world these days, I am seeing God's Spirit doing something wonderful in the hearts of believers everywhere. I'm seeing Him moving in a miraculous way in the lives of people who have been Christians for a long time, but they are hungering for more. They're tired of the stale routines they have experienced in their Christian life. They want to rise to a new level in both their walk with God and in the impact they are having on the world around them. Does that describe you? Explain it in your own words. What is God doing inside you in this area?

> *Intimacy with God isn't something that cuts us off from the rest of the world.*

_____

_____

_____

## A REVOLUTION IS BEGINNING

I just Googled "define: revolution" on the Internet and here's what popped up first: "1. A drastic and far-reaching change in ways of thinking and behaving; 2. The overthrow of a government by those who are governed." I see both of these happening in the Christian community today.

Many of us are seeing a change in the way we've thought about how we practice our faith. It's affecting our behavior too. We want more than the routine religious rituals we've lived with for many years. We aren't saying that everything about it is wrong. It's just that we want more in our experience than the same-old-same-old we've known for years.

Some things are wrong and need to be overturned. The prevailing viewpoint that God is more concerned about the behavior of His children than anything else is wrong. The common belief that God blesses us because of what *we* do is wrong. The practice of reaching out to certain types of people with the gospel while ignoring others is wrong. The list could go on. My intention isn't to be negative, but when we love health we have to hate disease and the disease of legalism has infected the church world.

The rule of legalism in God's church needs to be overturned. It has had the limelight long enough. It has been tried and found wanting. Many of us have determined to speak up for Christ and speak out against that which opposes Him from behind a religious mask. Revolution seems to be a good word to describe what God is doing among Christian these days.

For many years I lived in a religious mindset where my greatest concern was about *me* and how I behaved. In 1990, when I began to understand the grace walk, I started to learn that the Christian life isn't about what I do. Christianity is about what He has already done! In the years that have followed, as I have grown in intimacy with my God, I have experienced a growing hunger to make this message known.

> *The rule of legalism in God's church needs to be overturned.*

I know I'm not alone because I get email from people like you all the time. I meet them in conferences, churches, and small groups and even on airplanes. What I find is that they too want to do something to get the message of true grace out to the world. They're tired of the dry experience they've known for years, but they certainly aren't tired of Jesus. In fact, their passion for Him is growing every day. They want to make a meaningful spiritual difference on this planet. Whether they know it or not, they are a part of the early stages of a grace revolution that I believe is beginning in these last days.

Do you want to be a part of this revolution? It will emerge out of the very topic we have examined in this book for the past eight weeks ~ the love of God. I'm not so sure that the greatest potential for a mighty movement of God in our world during these last days requires "blatant sinners" to repent of their evil ways. The greatest catalyst for spiritual awakening on planet earth might happen if Christians would repent of their diluted and, consequently, polluted concept of the nature of God's love. What would happen if we were to really believe that God's love is indiscriminate and unconditional? Can you imagine the impact the gospel would have in the world when we began to share love from *that* viewpoint as we live our daily lives?

*Journey into Intimacy*

## LET'S DO IT

Here's a radical idea: Let's behave like Jesus, even if the Pharisees don't like it. Let's just love people indiscriminately. Let's love them regardless of their behavior. Let's love them whether they are pimps or preachers ~ whether they are crack-heads or corporate heads ~ whether they are drug addicts or deacons, whether they are moral or immoral. Let's just love them all!

Do you want to live the Christ life and be a part of the revolution of grace He wants to bring to His church and to the world? Then love people who may cause you to be criticized because you love them. Be radical about gracious love. Stop worrying about people thinking you are endorsing their sinful behavior. I can assure you that, given the judgmental attitude those trapped in sinful behavior see among many Christians, the likelihood that they will think you believe sin is okay is a very unlikely possibility.

When I one day considered the fact that Jesus was constantly criticized for loving the people He did, and realized that I had never, even once, been criticized for loving the wrong people, it pricked my heart. Not in a self-condemning way, but in a way that made me think, "I want to love people like Jesus does! I want to love indiscriminately and unconditionally!" Do you sense that desire too?

*Be radical about gracious love. Stop worrying about people thinking you are endorsing their sinful behavior.*

To join the revolution of grace is countercultural to the world of dead religion. To accept people wherever they are and love them the way Christ does is the outgrowth of intimacy with God. Do you recognize that to be true?

When we love people with the love of Christ, we may be surprised to see what happens in their lives. While we certainly don't condone sinful behavior, we must remember that we are expressing the love of the one "who came not into the world to condemn the world, but that the world through Him might be saved" (John 3:17). We neither condemn nor condone those who sin. We just love them as God loves them.

The increasing revelation of God's love to you will continue to bring transformation to your life. I encourage you to welcome the flow of living (and loving) water that is in you and flows through you to others. As His Life pours out of yours, everybody around you will get wet with the love of God!

*Week Eight*

Spend the rest of your life obsessed with your Father's love and He will use you to help change the world. Your Father's love is the most amazing thing in existence. It has transformed you and now, through you, it will transform others. Don't be embarrassed to act just like Him. What does it mean to be like Him?

He is the Father who falls on the neck of returning prodigals and with tears of joy streaming down His cheeks, kisses them and shouts with laughter, "My son is home! Let's have a party!" (See Luke 25:20-24) He is the Mother who smothers her babies in kisses as they snuggle against her breasts. (See Psalm 131:2) He is the Lover who says, "I love you so much that I'll kiss you right out in public and I don't care who sees me!" (See Song of Solomon 8:1) He is the Artist who points to you and declares proudly to the universe, "Look what I made!" (See Ephesians 2:10) He is the Composer who sings love songs to you. (See Zephaniah 3:17) He is the Wealthy Merchant who sold everything He had so that He could make you His own. (See Matthew 13:45-46) He is the King of kings and Lord of lords who left the glory of His exalted throne in heaven, waded through the filth of this sinful world, and descended into the horrors of hell ~ all for one simple reason. He looked beyond the horror and saw you standing on the other side, waiting for Him to rescue you.

> *Spend the rest of your life obsessed with your Father's love and He will use you to help change the world.*

What is your Father like? God is love. I encourage you to be who you are in Him. Love people. Just love them. Love them radically. You don't have to have an opinion about everything everybody else does. Just love them. You don't have to condone or condemn them. Just love them. Love them when they don't deserve it. Love them whether they act responsibly or repulsively. Just love them.

I pray that God will richly bless you as you continue forward on the road to intimacy. As you end your study today, write a prayer of thanksgiving in the space below for the things the Holy Spirit has shown you through this study. Ask Him to use you to share His love with other people. People everywhere are starving to be loved. You can meet that need. Ask Him to use you to do it.

*Dear Father,*

_____

_____

_____

_____

_____

_____

In Jesus name,

*Amen.*

# A Personal Word

Congratulations! You have completed an eight-week study on the topic of intimacy with God. The fact that you finished this shows that you have a sincere desire to experience and express your Father's love. That is a real evidence of the Holy Spirit working in your life.

It would be great to hear from you and to know how God used this book in your life. You can contact me at:

Dr. Steve McVey
Grace Walk Resources
PO Box 3669
Riverview, FL 33568

800-472-2311

Email: info@gracewalk.org

I also invite you to visit our web site at www.gracewalk.org to find out more about our ministry. You can find many other resources on our site that I have produced to further help you to grow in your own grace walk.

I mentioned in the final study in this book about being a part of "the growing grace revolution." Many of us are joining together in a united effort to make the message of God's amazing grace and unending love known across the world. We are doing this through our Grace Walk Groups Ministry. Small groups that are a part of our ministry are meeting in numerous countries in homes, churches, businesses and other locations, sharing the message of the grace walk.

If you have an interest in joining together with other grace walkers to be involved in this growing revolution of grace, I invite you to write me for more information. I provide ongoing training for those who want to be a facilitator of a Grace Walk Group. These leaders are an integral part of our ministry and are invited to private training sessions, retreats and other events not open to the public. If you have an interest in being a part of the Grace Walk team by being involved in this ministry effort, let me know. My goal is to see our Father bring about a groundswell revolution of grace through those of us who are united together to spread this message.

Thanks again for investing your time in this study. I hope that you and I will be able to meet one day soon. When we do, be sure to tell me that you've completed *Journey Into Intimacy*. May you be richly blessed as you continue onward.